First published in Great Britain in 2015 by
Pen & Sword Military
an imprint of
Pen & Sword Books Ltd
47 Church Street
Barnsley
South Yorkshire S70 2AS

Copyright © Barbara McClune 2015

ISBN 978 1 78346 369 5

The right of Barbara McClune to be identified as the Author of this Work has been asserted by her in accordance with the Copyright, Designs and Patents Act 1988

A CIP catalogue record for this book is available from the British Library

All rights reserved. No part of this book may be reproduced or transmitted in any form or by any means, electronic or mechanical including photocopying, recording or by any information storage and retrieval system, without permission from the Publisher in writing.

Typeset in Ehrhardt by
Mac Style Ltd, Bridlington, East Yorkshire
Printed and bound in China by Imago

Pen & Sword Books Ltd incorporates the imprints of Pen & Sword Archaeology, Atlas, Aviation, Battleground, Discovery, Family History, History, Maritime, Military, Naval, Politics, Railways, Select, Social History, Transport, True Crime, and Claymore Press, Frontline Books, Leo Cooper, Praetorian Press, Remember When, Seaforth Publishing and Wharncliffe.

For a complete list of Pen & Sword titles please contact
PEN & SWORD BOOKS LIMITED
47 Church Street, Barnsley, South Yorkshire, S70 2AS, England
E-mail: enquiries@pen-and-sword.co.uk
Website: www.pen-and-sword.co.uk

STAR SHELL REFLECTIONS 1914-19.

By JIM MAULTSAID

HAD … my first turn on sentry duty (24 hours). Lonely.

GOT … my regimental number 16873 today on 28 October 1914.

WAS … vaccinated 29 October. Awful; arm all swollen.

A … night march. All silence. A novelty, 4 November 1914.

FIERCE … firing heard here. Lasted two days. Came from Atlantic off Donegal coast, 6 and 7 November 1914.

AWFUL … weather for three days, 9 10 and 11 November. We were washed out. Tents blown away etc.

THEN … snow came. Very cold indeed, 15 November 1914.

HAD … great war games with the Skins.

STILL … the drilling goes on. From morn till night.

YES! … form fours [until 1937 British soldiers paraded four abreast]. Slope arms. Stand at ease, Skins.

FIRED … my first shots today, 27 November. Result good.

ROUTE … march. Eighteen miles. A great test. We stuck it.

DID … not fancy some of the old soldiers in Battalion.

PACKED … up and left canvas home for GNR Hotel.

FROM … 7 December until the 12th covered seventy-four miles. Marching.

10 … days' leave at Xmas. A great holiday.

6 January 1915. Goodbye to Finner. Off to Antrim.

WOOD … huts. Some change for us. A good camp.

25… miles route march. 9.00am until 8.00pm. Fine.

My chums were: W. Kelly, W. E. Reid, D. Figgens, John Towe, J. Montgomery, A. Mulholland, George Montgomery, W. Gray, T. Rooney, J. Rogers, J. Jackson, E .Savage, A. Miles, E. Powell, G. Mitchell, T. Wortley, J. Diamond, R. Black, S. Black, T. McClay, E. Gordon, Dae Mitchell, Lieutenant Monard, Lieutenant Wedgewood, etc.

WORK … at this camp is bayonet fighting, route marches, sham battles (blank cartridges), manoeuvres, running, boxing, and football.

GOT … my full equipment on 27 February 1915. The complete kit weighs about 80lbs.

BRIGADE … route march. Twenty-six miles. Full kit. A scorcher.

SAINT … Patrick's Day, 17 March 1915. Sports meeting. Got first prize for full race. Prize 15/- [fifteen shillings, 75p].

ROUTE … march to Ballymena. Full Brigade. Gee!

SOME OF MY CHUMS

J. TOWE. (KILLED)

D. FIGGINS (WOUNDED)

J. DIAMOND.

W. KELLY. (WOUNDED)

A. MULHOLLAND (DIED FROM WOUNDS)

W. GRAY. (WOUNDED)

J. JACKSON (WOUNDED)

W. REID. (KILLED)

A. MILLS. (WOUNDED)

JOSEPH MONTGOMERY. (KILLED)

GEORGE MONTGOMERY. (WOUNDED)

CAPT. WILLIS. (MISSING)

BILLY MAULTSAID (WOUNDED)

DOT. MAULTSAID. (KILLED)

MY PICTURE GALLERY.

FIRST … stripe. Now a full blown Lance Corporal. I felt some boy now, 20 April. Number one step.

ANOTHER … march to Castledawson, 28 April; a great day.

SOME … big day this, 8 May 1915. Ulster Division in full war paint. Marched all the way from Randalstown to Belfast for review. Some twenty thousand troops on parade. The pride of old Ulster. Fine troops. Felt a glow of pride as we passed the hundreds of thousands of spectators.

GETTING … back from Belfast, fought a sham battle on our way back near Antrim. The North Irish Horse and Inniskilling Dragons took part. My company, D, built a bridge during the night under orders from Royal Engineers, all in silence and near enemy.

THE Y.C.V'S IN THE BIG PARADE MAY 1915.

OUR … brigade was 109. Made up as follows: 9th Battalion Inniskillings (Tyrone), 10th Battalion, Skins, (Derry); 11th Battalion Skins (Donegal and Fermanagh) and 14th Royal Irish Rifles (Belfast). The Skins were great boys and we got along fine. Our best chums were the Derry lot.

GREAT … 25 May 1915. I had a field day [and] won several events 100 … 200 and NCOs' race, also a couple of inter-company relay and battalion events. Good money prizes.

NEWS … of a move to England. Can it be true? Getting near our ambition now. We are tired of training and want the real stuff.

LEFT … Randalstown on 6 July 1915 for somewhere in England. Our route was via Dublin and Holyhead, then right down through England via London to land in Seaford on the south coast. A little seaside spot in Sussex. The inhabitants were a bit scared at first of the wild Irishmen, about twenty-five thousand or so.

WHEN … I stood on the troopship and watched the shores of auld Ireland grow dim, it brought a lump to my throat. Perhaps I would never see them again? Who knows?

WE … can hear the big gunfire from across the Channel. I can picture our troops over there. Only wish I could help.

THE … first airship I ever set eyes on passed out to sea over our camp on 9 July 1915, but was later in the day towed back to harbour by a warship. A big biplane passed over on same date.

36TH … Division inspected by General Archibald on 14 and 15 July. We were highly complimented.

WERE … inspected by the great Lord Kitchener himself on 20 July. Pleased? He was delighted with us. Do coming events cast their shadows before? Are we for foreign service?

ON … 17 July two RE [Royal Engineers] men drowned. Sad day in camp. Some of our battalion put in fine rescue work.

I … made sixty-three points out of sixty-five at rifle range. Was always a good shot and handy with a gun.

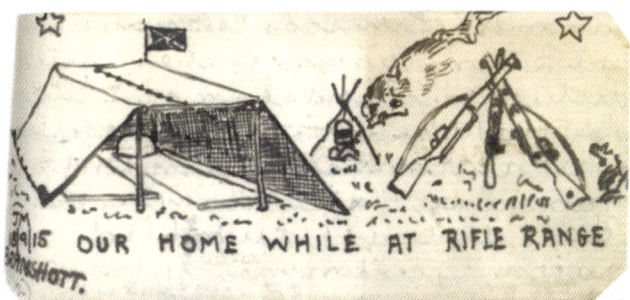

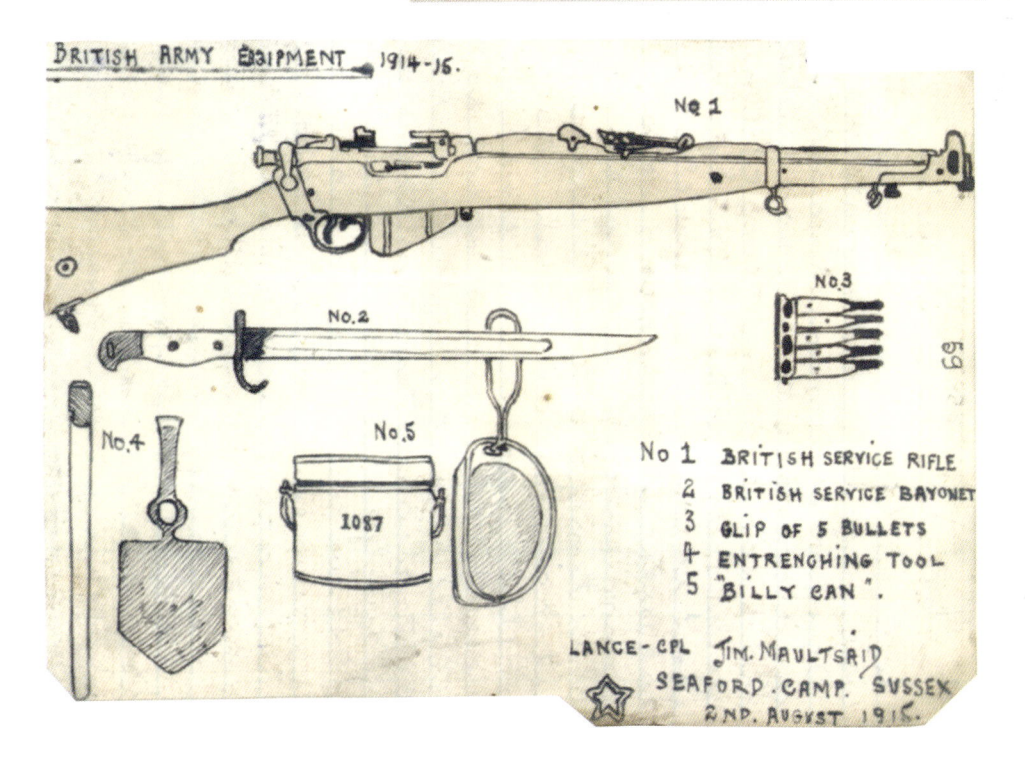

OUR HOME WHILE AT RIFLE RANGE

BRITISH ARMY EQUIPMENT 1914-15.

No 1 BRITISH SERVICE RIFLE
2 BRITISH SERVICE BAYONET
3 CLIP OF 5 BULLETS
4 ENTRENCHING TOOL
5 "BILLY CAN".

LANCE-CPL JIM. MAULTSAID
SEAFORD . CAMP. SUSSEX
2ND. AUGUST 1915.

SIR ... Edward Carson paid us a visit on 5 August. He said K of K [Kitchener of Khartoum] told him we were far too good to be at home.

REVIEWED ... by General Dickson on 18 August 1915. Good report.

TRAINING ... here was fierce. Trench digging. Night marches. Skirmish and tactical work. Real soldiering now.

PICKED ... as bomber [grenades were known as bombs] to represent D Company. Was delighted. This was my natural outlet.

I WAS ... trained with several chums for sports meeting in London. Was taken for guard night before event and missed it. All my chums won their events and I could have beaten any of them. Cruel luck!

LEFT ... Seaford for Bramshott on advance guard, 31 August. Nice spot. The camp was filthy; we spent days scraping and washing the hut floors. The previous division were a dirty lot and no error. Work now is all bombing. We make real-life bombs and can throw as only Belfast men know how. Lieutenant Wright was in charge. He is popular.

JUST ... a year [in] the army today, 14 September 1915. Feeling fine, fit and well. Should have been in France long ago, but this is beyond me.

HAD ... a week on rifle range at Little Dean. Had to camp out under little shelters made by ourselves. Went through full course of musketry with our little short Lee-Enfield rifles [the Short Magazine Lee-Enfield rifle, known as the SMLE, was coming into service].

GOT ... last leave before departure for foreign lands, 18 to 22 September. Goodbye now to all our loved ones – then off we go.

ON 30 September reviewed by King George V. All complete. Ready for the fray, our artillery attached, also transport etc. We gave a great reception, that only Irish men could give. 'The Day' looms near.

OFF AT LAST ... 3 October 1915. Bustle, packing, cleaning then 'fall in'. Hurrah! We are off now. Down to Southampton and on board the big transport ship. Is it France or abroad? No one knows. Who cares! We move out in the dark, in silence, not a friend to say farewell. How lonely I feel, but hundreds like me. The last sound I heard was a shout from shore 'Go on the Blues'. [The Blues are Linfield FC] Can you beat it?

THE 14TH ROYAL IRISH RIFLES (YCV)

Landed in France on 4 October 1914.

Our trials, sorrows and triumphs can be followed through these pages.

KITCHENER SPEAKS

Did our boys keep these instructions?

WISE WORDS from the great man himself. They are cut from my pay-book – and I always treasured them. Did our boys keep them? Yes! Ninety-nine per cent of them did. The Ulster boys did not let their Province down. No finer division ever landed on the shores of France, and no more God-fearing troops ever took the field – clean upright fellows. The few samples (photographs) surely speak for themselves, a fair example of our lads who went out to face the Huns in 1915. We certainly did not let our big chief down either, as everywhere we went it was a case of making friends – and upholding the honour of the British Soldier.

HERE WE ARE

WHERE ARE WE?
This was the question on all sides as our big transport churned its way alongside the quayside. Sleepy heads looked out from port-holes. Somewhere in France? Not yet, but close up anyhow. My first glimpse of this strange land was a long line of sheds and French soldiers in red (yes, red) trousers, strolling up and down, with a long rifle slung on their shoulder. No doubt now in my mind. This was the French soldier as per the textbook come to life. But where was it? Orders to fall in cut short our dreams and brought our stiff joints into action. We were stiff and sore all over. Days in trains, lying in sheds at Southampton, then crushed and cramped in the hold of the ship made us half doped – wake up there! What a voice that sergeant has! As a good lance corporal I mustered my section and obeyed the command.

WE GET THERE
Down the gangways we swarmed. By the right – quick – march. The band crashed out and away we went. All was very strange to us. Funny houses. Funny shops. Oh! The old tramcars.

RAIN – RAIN – THEN MORE!
How it rained. Soaked in a short time, this was a miserable start to a new life. At last we reached camp. Tents and mud. Ah! That mud. The usual stuff in unloading stores, rations, etc., etc. Fatigue parties galore. Bully beef, biscuits and tea for dinner, then more hard graft.

We had now discovered le Havre. A dull drab place, and it still rained. Night falls, we sink down on our equipment in the mud. Yes! Six inches of black, black mud. What a life. Weary, tired, miserable, the night passed. Sprawled over each other as we were twenty or twenty-five to each tent, sleep was simply a nightmare.

OFF AGAIN
Reveille had us up with the lark. Scraping and washing kit and ourselves occupied a good part of the morning.

> Would we soon get moved on?
> We all hoped so anyhow.
> It would be better out in the open. Hurrah! News of the shift. Good.
> Pack up again, fall in and goodbye to le Havre.

A long line of railway trucks. Strange looking to us. Marked twenty hommes. Men this meant, so our French experts (or supposed experts) said. Embark boys. No carriages here. Just ordinary trucks, but welcome.

UP THE LINE

SPEED, BUT NOT FOR US

How the boys kidded about the speed of our train. You could have got out to pick flowers along the line. Not so bad as all that, but crawling along at about 10mph is a good estimate. We sat with our legs swinging out. We played cards. We smoked. We sang the hours away, and ever onwards crawled nearer the front. About a day and a half of this, past little wayside stations we had a good view of France, then into a fair-sized station (now night-time) and the order came: Get out! Out we got. Formed up and away we went through the town.

WELCOME

Despite the lateness of the hour there were quite a lot of onlookers. French lassies threw windows open and shouted strange words of welcome to us. Threw kisses too, and of course we replied. Much kidding and banter passed. This was Amiens, the city of a fine cathedral and my only view [of it] during my service in France.

WERE WE LOST?

Tramped for hours (so I thought) around this village. By the way, our official interpreter disappeared here. Did he go on his own or was he dismissed? Anyhow, to the best of my knowledge I never set eyes on him again. Was he a spy?

SCROUNGING

Still marching! Lost? It felt like it, and I swear we passed the same place several times. Grousing was common now amongst the troops. At last we cut out to the countryside along a straight road, all trees on each side, halted at a little village that was to be our first billet in the new land. A big barn was my home. No straw or anything else, so my one and only official 'scrounger' (this is a slang word for getting things in some way for nothing) went forth on his errand. The goods were found. We sank down, weary and exhausted to sleep, the sleep of the just and the unjust. Out to the world!

BAD DREAMS – OR BAD DRINK?

Next morning, or rather that same morning, as I had to shift my digs, my section and I were moved to a little house that ran alongside a graveyard. In fact to me it was the 'dead house'. Still, it was clean and neat, so that was something, and the cold did not blow through it, like the big barn.

I GET PROMOTION

Lieutenant Monard informed me that I was now Corporal Maultsaid. When I got my first stripe I was taken from Lieutenant Wedgewood (much to my sorrow; he was only seventeen or so and we were great friends). Since that time I was under Lieutenant Monard and although I did not agree in many ways with his style I admired him. 'Corporal Jim, you and I are now going to be fast friends?' 'Yes sir!' We shook hands and sealed the bargain.

LIEUTENANT MONARD

What staunch friends we were too. From that day, and ever since. He was a real active service officer and loved his Irish boys. A Londoner by birth, his opinion of these Irishmen was immense.

WHITE SHADOWS

'Say Corporal, did you see the ghosts last night?' Tommy Rooney asks the question and Tommy was a real old-fashioned Catholic. 'I'm afraid my boy that bad 'vin blong' [vin blanc: white wine] I stood you lads yesterday has affected you.' 'Well just ask Rogers or McClay.' I did so. Yes! Sure as a gun they swore that a figure or two had appeared late last night behind the wall of the graveyard. White shrouds too, all complete.

REVENGE!

I knew there was something afoot that night, but turned a blind eye. Starting up from a drowsy sleep I heard the most awful racket. Hastened outside as all the noise was coming from amongst the gravestones. Getting a grip on the wall I clambered up. As I did so, two heavy black bundles were dropped over, then half the platoon jumped over too. 'What the H****'s all this?' I shouted. 'Here's the ghosts, Corporal.' Sure enough they were material beings and not spiritual.

Two of the boys had discovered an underground vault leading from our billet right under the wall and into the graveyard. This gave rise to a fine chance for some fun. Getting two white sheets by some means from the cookhouse they played this trick and put the wind up No. 14 Platoon. Then a few others found the passage and sheets. Formed a vengeance party, kept it quiet, lay and watched the two lads slip down the vault. Gave them time, then silently followed. My word, those youths got shocks, in fact they were 'outed' for the count and dropped over the wall to be slowly revived by throwing cold water over them. No more 'white shadows' troubled us. We kept the joke to ourselves.

MY FIRST FRENCH FRIENDS

Once more on the move. Swinging along in fine style we put many kilometres behind us. Hard as nails, our lot could march some and it was looked upon as a kind of disgrace to fall out.

Packs, rifles and ammunition got very heavy, how the shoulder straps cut into our poor shoulders, but an old song in which we all chimed in, gave us new heart to struggle on. By the way our Battalion had some of the finest singers in the 36th Division, each platoon having a fair share and D Company some of the best. Poor old D Company, last of the line, often bent, but never broken. Always last, but often first if you can grasp the Irish here.

The weather was bad. Cold wet and conditions wretched as we plodded along.

FRIENDS OF MINE

The lights of a fair sized town greeted us and we found ourselves in Beauval. Halt! Fall out. Dismiss. As I made my way to our allotted billet a little French boy caught me by the sleeve and whispered milk and 'du pang' (du pain: bread). All right sonny, wait a minute. Getting my section fixed up I followed my guide and was led to his home. Poor people. Father, mother, young son and young daughter (both kiddies) all gave me a welcome in French. It was awkward, but by signs, much gesticulating and other means, we got along splendidly.

Their eldest boy had given his life for his country and they were determined to do all in their power for his 'comrades' as they termed us. I was asked, 'Are your boys all Catholic soldiers?' 'No! Most of my lot are Protestants.' An awful surprise this as all Irish soldiers were put in the Catholic category. Then what joy when it transpired that this family were of the same faith. A big Bible was produced and we all looked over it. The one and only lot of Protestants I ever met on my travels around France and Belgium.

A LITTLE GIFT

A bottle of milk and a long loaf were pressed on me, so of course I had to be friendly and accept the gift. During our few days' stay I was a welcome guest at this humble home. How I enjoyed it all, but the day of departure came and I said goodbye, never to meet these friends again.

Star Shell Reflections 1914–1916

FACING GERRY SHAKING

DRAWN IN FRANCE

PICTURES FROM MY STORY "FACING JERRY"

STAR SHELL DISPLAY JERRYS NIGHT TURN.

A HOPELESS TASK FIGHTING THE MUD

ALL BEFORE US LAY THE FRONT LINE TRENCHES A WONDERFUL VIEW — STAR SHELLS AND ROCKETS LIT UP THE SCENE

WHAT THE GERMAN FRONT LINE LOOKED LIKE. MY FIRST VIEW FROM 200 YARDS RANGE.

MY FIRST SHOT — AT STAND-TO.

NOT TOO BAD. THE ROOF HAS GONE — THESE POOR PEOPLE HELD ON TO THE LAST MOMENT.

Maison de la Somme détruite par les obus allemands | House destroyed by german shells in the Somme

SKETCHES FROM MY WAR DAIRY RE-DRAWN LINE FOR LINE AS PER THE ORIGINAL IN PENCIL. J.M. 1916.

The dust of Beauval from our feet (or mud) we started that last journey that was to find us opposite the Germans and, to me, this was a most momentous of moments. How I had pictured it all. The darkness, the silence and the pad of feet.

INTO THE WAR ZONE
Marching all day we passed some signs and tokens of war. The country round about us was deserted and you could have felt the nearness of things unnatural. What's that?

In the far distance we heard Boom! Boom! Guns! Big stuff too. Yes! Getting there now.

COMPLETE SILENCE
A little wood with some tents. We rested for the night. Silence complete. This was too close for much noise. Up at dawn and off again. A march this that I cannot somehow properly describe. Suffice it to say that nightfall found us at the edge of the communication trenches. Rest! Down go our tired bodies in the mud, equipment and all. The ground slopes downward in front of us, as we lay we could see the star shells in various colours light up the sky. How strange it all felt. The guns added their part to the general scheme of things.

THE GUNS GROWL
A whispered command. We pulled our bodies from that everlasting mud and the final stage commenced. Splash! The man in front of me falls into something and I slide in after him. Snakes alive! It's the trenches now. Wet, damp earth on each side and over the shoes, mouth in water. Gee! This feels like prison. Like a rat in a trap. Ping – Zipp! zip! zip! Whizz – bang. Just a welcome from Fritz.

Peculiar is the only word I know to explain my innermost feelings. Sliding, slipping with a muffled curse now and again we are in the 'firing line' now. Muffled figures greet us with 'Are you Irish chum?' 'Yes! Sure we are, what's your lot?'

THE TERRIERS
'The Warwicks' (Terriers, or Territorials, of the Territorial Force) Good enough. 'Look here, Corporal. Get two men for this sap. Three for this post and one here. Now, come along and we will put you wise.' All the posts were double strength that night as our chums had us for instruction. Fine fellows, too. In fact I met many Englishmen in later days but none could hold a candle to these lads. Our rucksacks (or packs) were dumped in little dug-outs, little holes only that held four or five, some below the floor level of trench and some cut in the side of trench with a blanket as a door. Strange world this!

LEARNING TRENCH LORE
Question, answer, question and answer went on all night. We were out to learn. 'Two hundred yards or so, just over there chum and Jerry faces you,' and this was the Somme front. 'Are you boys long out? Yes! Too dammed long, Pat. Fed up.' Oh what a life!

HAVE YOU EVER MET THE DAWN?
It was intensely interesting all this to us. Night slowly faded away. The dawn comes. Did you ever sit up and meet the Dawn? No! Well, try it sometime. It was awe-inspiring. The bullets began to whizz overhead. 'Keep low, Pat.' Jerry wakes up.

GREETINGS
Stand to! Bleary-eyed, tired, sleepy khaki forms crawled out from dug-outs and bunk holes to take their place on the fire-step and send the morning's greetings across no man's land.

MY FIRST SHOT
Slipping a clip of cartridges into my well-oiled magazine I shut the breech and, getting up, peeped between two wet sandbags to get my first look at the enemy trenches. To me it appeared to be a long white line of chalk with a wood of skeleton trees behind and on top of a slight rise. So this was my objective. Taking steady aim I pressed the trigger and fired my first shot.

DIP BREAD AND BACON
Here comes breakfast chum. My pal the Corporal from Birmingham touched me on the arm. Tea, dipped bread, some fat bacon and it's all over. Wonderful how a drop of tea takes that low-down sinking feeling from the pit of one's stomach.

REST?
A spell 'off duty' allowed me to crawl into my dug-out to forget all about war for a few hours.

OUR FIGHT WITH THE MUD
Two hours on. Four off. Duty off and on. We fought the mud with big ladles, buckets and hand pumps. All no use. It's up to [our] knees in parts, sticks like glue.

Many friendships were formed with our Warwick comrades.

ARTILLERY ACTIVITY
Our artillery put in a good spell of shelling practically all day of our third day in the front line. This seemed a lot for them as four or five shells per gun was a good day's average early in the war for British artillery. We peeped out to watch our shells burst on the enemy parapets.

BEWARE RESULTS
A little notice on a board 'BEWARE – dangerous spot' made me curious. Popping up to glance over almost cost me my life. A bullet smashed through as I got down to sink into the clay at the back of trench. A narrow shave. That bullet is in my possession to this day.

HYMNS FROM THE AIR

Sunday morning still found us in the trenches. This was our last day and completed one week's duty.

PRAISING THE LORD

I have it recorded that early on this Sabbath morn we were astonished to hear the singing of hymns and playing of concertinas in perfect harmony from across no man's land. What do you think of that? Needless to say we did not interrupt as this was a sacred time for them (the enemy) and like ourselves they believed in God, not being afraid to praise him even in the front-line trenches.

RELIEF ... AND REST?

That night found our relief battalion at our side taking over our duties. A tired, weary, unshaven lot of boys splashed down the communication trench covered with a coat of black mud, glad of the prospect of a good wash, a sleep in peace and some rest ... but wait! Did I say rest? Perish the thought.

BILLETS AND REST?

Out for a rest sounds nice enough, but if ever a word was murdered it was the word 'rest' during the war. Sometimes it was better in the line than out of it.

CLEANING UP THE MESS

Parade at 8.00am, spotlessly clean! Just think of it. How were we to get the dirt off? It had to be done. Belts, straps and all were dipped into the village pond (every village in France has a pond of dirty, evil-smelling water somewhere). The jack knife scraped the mud off. Dried and greased, it was marvellous the change that came over our equipment. Next our boots, puttees, pants and great coats were tackled to produce a spick and span soldier once more. All this meant up about 5.30am to get it accomplished.

APPLES ARE SWEET – WHEN YOU CAN GET THEM

'Home' now was a little ruined village some six or seven kilometres behind the line. One or two old French people still live here. No young men, just old men and women. Guards and sentries fixed, most of us had time for some fun. A funny incident that happened here comes to my mind. Some of the lads discovered a nice big orchard that looked inviting.

A QUICK DESCENT

Up the trees they swarmed and were busily picking off big red rose-coloured apples when – BANG! BANG! FLASH! Fast as lightning came those shells. What a sight! Ye gods! The boys drop down like sacks of coal from the branches and dashed for cover. No one hurt? No! How we laughed afterwards.

THE RATION PARTY

Ration parties wanted. The next worry. Corporal Maultsaid and twenty men will parade at 10.00pm. Sandbags containing bread, bully beef etc. were loaded on us and away we went back up the old trail again to report at a certain dump. This was practically an all-night job. We found ourselves back home in the early hours, in bad temper as it had rained all the time and we were wet to the skin again. An old brazier was lit up and clothes laid out to dry on the floor. Crawling between a couple of old army blankets, we were asleep from exhaustion in a few minutes.

THE RATION PARTY.

Jim. Maultsaid — 1916 —

Above picture is a fine example of the ration party going up with supplies. Note rum jars across a pole. And the mud! Bah! I can taste it yet — yes taste it!

SWEEPING THROUGH FRANCE

Road-sweeping fatigue party 'fall in', here goes a fine job. Brushes, shovels issued at QM's [Quarter-Master's] store. 'Report to Sergeant so and so.' The village streets and square were well swept. If we had been there a few more years I think there would not have been a road left in France unswept.

THE BOMBING PATROL

VOLUNTEER section wanted from each company – 'must be BOMBERS', wanted for a spell of instruction in the front line. Rapidly making up my mind I volunteered for the work. Several of my chums did likewise and we got our orders to report at a village called Auchonvillers. We eventually arrived at this miserable spot, one of the most forsaken places to my mind I ever came across on my travels around the battle fronts; there was something about it I did not like.

ALL COMRADES – THE RIFLES MEET
Each battalion of the Rifles seems to be represented here on this errand. My section leader was a Sergeant Hunter from the 10th Battalion (South Belfast), a fine chap indeed, also a fearless one. We were a mixture of privates, corporals and lance corporals. Mills bombs were served out and off we set for the front line. A long bare road led up to the communication trench and it was a wet miserable winter's night when we began our tramp.

THE MAD HORSES PASS … A NARROW ESCAPE
Hark, what is that? Startled, we paused in our stride as the sound that came to our ears was nothing that we could explain. Horses' hooves? Yes! By G★★, and, mad with fear, that whirlwind was amongst us. Six big chargers with eyes staring out, galloping all out, with the drivers hanging on like grim death, the gun and limber thundering behind, all and everyone helpless.

We simply hurled ourselves to the roadside into the mud and out of the way. My! I'll never forget that sight as the lights from the battlefront lit up the scene. It was like a bad dream that passed.

What happened to them I know not, as our business was to get forward.

INTO THE UNKNOWN
Final instructions, then up over the parapet just a few minutes past midnight. The snow was coming. It was bitterly cold. No rifles now, but big six-shooters and bombs in each pocket. Before we ventured out each man blackened his face and left all papers behind for fear of capture.

Through our wire carefully, each one of us fully alert now. How odd it felt. The long grass up to our knees, the shell holes we stumbled into, and our own hearts pounding like steam hammers. What's that? A black object looms up and I flatten out as I never did before – well, like lightning – was it moving? I'll swear it did, but that must be a big German surely! My finger gripped the trigger of my gun. Then a star shell relieved our feelings: it was the stump of a tree, and, strange to say, we had all been on the same track, surrounding it. How the cold bites. My teeth chattering. Excitement runs high as we crawl on our bellies across no man's land.

AT THE GERMAN WIRE
Nearer and nearer to the big dark line of enemy wire we move.

I touch it. Feel the barbs. My, it's thick stuff. Face downwards, ears to the ground we listened for Jerry. Splash! Splash! Muffled voices. A sentry being relieved? If they only knew we were so close. Not twenty yards away I would say. But our orders were 'look out and intercept enemy patrols only,' so we slid along through the wet grass on our tummies.

Again and again I said to myself 'this is my life now'. And it was: all my life I have been interested in Scouts and scouting – Buffalo Bill stories in my young days had fired my blood and I often trailed and tracked small birds and animals (rabbits etc.). This was the real thing now, no mistake.

Flares from friend and foe worried us. When they flared up we stood or crouched – stood still as death. To have moved would have meant a stream of machine-gun bullets and death perhaps.

NERVES
Jerry had one or two bad attacks of nerves and banged away for several minutes at a stretch. Strange to lie and watch the flashes stabbing the darkness. This would die down.

RETURN JOURNEY
A whispered command was passed along and the journey homewards commenced. How long it took I cannot say.

SNOW – AND – WIRE
Big snowflakes falling fast.
    Curse that wire of ours.
    My foot caught, but wisely I kept cool and gradually released myself. Worming our way in, we slid past our sentries after giving the password 'Sandy Row'.
    My first patrol was over. I felt happy and proud.
    Not being liable for trench duty, we made our way back a little to crawl in and rest our bodies in a fairly large dug-out. How sweet it was to see the candle burn, get a Dixie full of hot tea and lie down.

MORE TO COME
My dreams were all about stalking Germans.
    Six nights of this work made us very cute in many ways. Our adventures would fill a book. I'll give you some later.

GAS
According to my notebook we had our first experience of real gas with helmets on by passing through one door and out by another of the chamber filled with the real stuff. Quite a novelty this, knowing an error on your part might mean a life of misery, but so far as I know none of our lads were unduly affected. I may say now that I was fortunate in never coming through or having to face a real gas attack; I did not fancy it much.

THE FIRST GAS ATTACK
It was a terrible surprise the first gas attack against our troops and almost lost us that part of the line but the usual British soldiers' pluck stood up to it and we weathered the storm (or cloud). Gas helmets were unknown to our boys then and a story that was told me will give you some idea of the terrible ordeal they passed through.
    'Say Mac that's a funny smell – and oh my G★★ my throat is on fire! Gasping, choking, tears ran down our faces as we pulled at our tunics and shirts to open the neck bands. How our lungs contracted and our breath came in short sharp gasps. Some of our men collapsed, some went mad almost and others choked out their life's blood.'

A DRASTIC REMEDY

'Quick as a thought the fire brigade came into my mind' (this is my informant now speaking) 'and dashing for a urinal bucket I dashed an old handkerchief into it and wrapped it around my mouth and nose.

'Did it save my life? Well! I'm here yet as you can see, but still troubled with my chest sir! Poor fellows they came through the mill.

The Germans followed up their gas with an attack, but our boys beat them off and it's suspected they fell into their own trap as the gas veered around owing to the wind and hampered them.'

ALL FOR ONE 1/- PER DAY.
7.A.M.
SHAVE.
'SHUN!
"EASY"
ON THE RIGHT-HOP.
LUNGE
MARCH
SLOPE ARMS.
FIX BAYONETS.
ABOUT TURN.
BLANKET FATIGUE.
ON GUARD
9.P.M.
DRAWN BY JIM MAULTSAID -1914-

GAS HELMETS INVENTED

After this our people got busy to evolve some protection. You can see their efforts in my sketches a few pages from this. The first attempts were crude, but eventually our gas mask was one of the best amongst the Allied armies; in fact it beat them all, friend and foe.

OLD STYLE GAS MASKS.

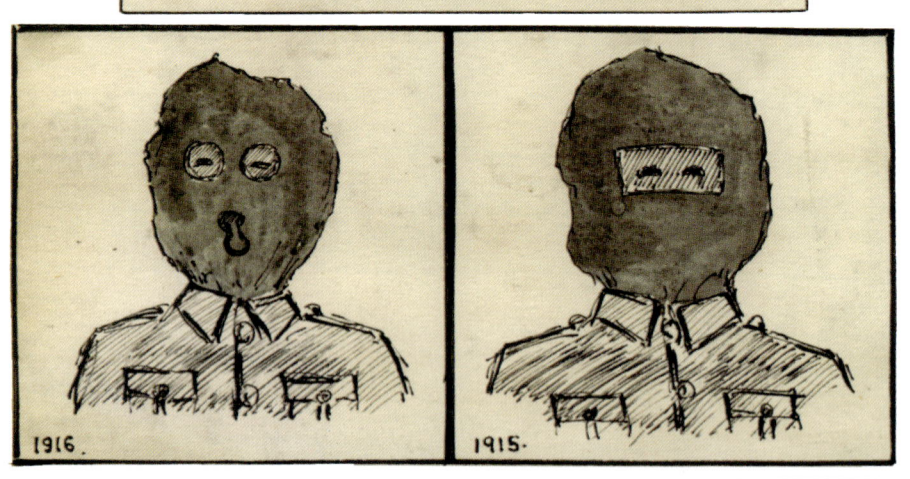

1916.   1915.

In the little cottage of a poor Flanders peasant sits a mother with her child, both of them wearing the gas-masks which are an absolute necessity for everybody within reach of the mephitic vapours of the Hun

NO MORE GAS?
A horrible mode of warfare.
   One that I hope and trust will never again be tried. This wish is futile I know that no matter what laws are drawn up amongst the nations, these can and will be treated as a scrap of paper when it suits them.

VERMIN

Just about this time I began to feel ill at ease. I itched and on the quiet scratched myself, but did not admit to myself that I was simply in a torment and 'walking away'.

Seeing my chums in the same condition it gave me heart to mention the fact that I was 'lousy', covered indeed with fleas, or bugs if you like. Crude language this, but grim and true.

We killed them. We boiled our shirts and vests. Washed our bodies in all kinds of disinfectants – all no use.

I think the little beggars laid eggs under our skin and hatched them too.

Strange to say the bloodless kind of men were not attacked in any degree of discomfort, but as for me – well, I put in a bad time of it, the good red blood in my veins was to their liking.

WIPING OUT THE ~ PESTS ~

RELIEF AT LAST

I tried an experiment once and it was a relief. Each soldier had two shirts. My plan was to pick out a spot in or near the billet when out of the trenches, dig a hole, take off my shirt and bury it. Next time that way, I dug up the spot again, got the article, washed it and, lo, I had some relief. Of course it did not always work out and many a shirt I lost, having to buy another to replace it in kit, but it was worth it all.

RATS – RATS – AND THEN RATS

You will perhaps have noticed that up to now I have not mentioned our old friends the 'rats'. Well they were plentiful enough. In the line it simply swarmed with them and the dug-outs had their hundreds and thousands of these visitors. It gave you a funny kind of feeling down your spine to strike up a light in the underground passages and see all those little dots of sparkling flame glare out at you from all the corners and crevices, their eyes shining in the half darkness. Then a scurry off.

We walked over them often. This was unpleasant and it was worse to wake up from a doze to feel them scamper over your face. Ah! It was horrible but we got used to it all.

I remember one part of the line we were in and, oh my!, they were fat. Big stomachs. Good food somewhere, but certainly not any surplus from us as we had little enough ourselves. The only explanation I could think of was the line ran through what had at one time been a large country estate and the partridges flopped about in large numbers. Did our friends live on these? I think they did.

FIGHTING THE VERMIN

SNIPING

A few bits of cheese on the point of your bayonet as bait and sure as fate they came! Bang! Bang! Bang! Two more out of the way. It took it all to keep them down. Dogs and cats were useless here.

A fine pastime. For a bet of a franc or so we often sat around a candle, and took off our shirts and commenced the hunt for little pests. A time limit of ten minutes was laid down and the winner was the man who caught the most. Not a nice pleasant subject to talk about, but true to life and often played by No.14 Platoon with grim and determined earnestness.

AND THE MUD!

Green – yellow and black.

Should I write from now until the crack of doom I could not say by half all I should about this commodity. We lived in it, we ate in it and we died in it. Bah! It was sickening.

We fought it – yes! And often beat it, but always back it came. There was mud in all colours – green – yellow and black. There was mud that stuck like glue, there was stuff like cement and there was the kind that sickened you by its odour. Ah!

That everlasting mud, at times it made life a nightmare and to escape we often climbed over our own parapets out amongst the wire and death, in the darkness, anything for relief.

DOWN! DOWN! IN THE MUD

It was not uncommon to rescue a chum from death by slow drowning in this slime. The French troops had a rare idea of digging drainage or sump-holes in the [path] way of their trenches, then placing a trench board over it. Quite good enough until the water came up and the mud formed and away floated the plank. This left a regular death trap of about six or seven feet to allow our boys to fall in. Of course it was not intended thus, but it often happened and we 'fell' for it until we got wise – wise after a bath in black cold mud and filthy water.

HOW WE LOVED THE MOTOR CONVOYS

Rest camps, billets, horse and transport lines were all the same in winter time. Body and soul were often tired out in dragging ourselves through it.

On the march the poor infantryman suffered. A big convoy of motor lorries splashed, splashed, splashed it up and around us. Don't you remember how we love those convoys?

UP IT CAME – OOZING UP
Sweeping, scraping and piling it up was a daily routine. Old tins were used to make paths. Tree branches, crossed and re-crossed, were laid down, stones, rubble and anything we could lay our hands on filled in the holes, but still it oozed up and over.

A PATH LAID WITH OLT JAM TINS – BULLY BEEF TINS AND BRANCHES. TO TRY AND BEAT THE MUD.

JIM. MAULTSAID. 1915.

EVERYWHERE – MUD! MUD! MUD!
Mud! Mud! Mud! D *** it!

To the day I die I will never forget that blasted stuff.

It worked its way into our food. The loaf was often covered in it. I suppose I had my share.

Rifles were bandaged at the muzzles and breaches, old socks were used, but in it crept. Nothing on earth could have kept it out. It was everywhere, stuck to us and we stuck to it. Awful stuff!

FUN AND FROLICS

It must not be thought that our life out here is all 'work' and no play. Far from it. Sport and games, not to mention concerts, were all encouraged. It was found that this took our minds from the grimness of it all and made us 'forget' ourselves, if only for an hour or so. This was often a source of much wonderment to the French people who often looked on, shook their heads and said in dumb language – mad! – mad!

15 PLATOON: 3 – 14 PLATOON: 0

A note in my little book reads … No.14 Platoon got beaten 3 - 0 today (this on 16 November 1915) by our old enemy No.15 Platoon. Football! Yes, a great game, played by us on every available chance.

Two uprights made from tree branches, cord across a crossbar and a ball from the lord - knows - where. We did not spare ourselves. The inter-platoon, inter-company rivalry was simply fierce. No game for a weakling! Get out or get under. How the men love to meet the NCOs, but whisper, those men did not always win; no my lad – they did not. Those boys holding stripes could play a little too, and boot just as well as the men. Bet your life, we didn't take it lying down. No! Siree!

BOXING

Boxing found a place. This was a game I loved and always welcomed a round or two with anyone willing enough. You will find my history in the roped square on other pages in this book. My great friend in this line was Jim Magee, a born gentleman. Big Jim was a heavyweight, but as gentle as a lamb. Everyone loved him, you simply could not help yourself.

OLD FAVORITES

Sing-songs were popular. Talent was plentiful. How the lads sang and played 'The Mountains of Mourne', 'Bridget Lie close to the Wall', 'Pack all your Troubles, etc., etc.', 'Only one more Kit Inspection, Only one more Church Parade', 'Mademoiselle from Armentières'. They all got a turn on the platform and at private platoon or company sing-songs. It sometimes made me sad to listen to it all. I was a poor singer, but enjoyed it.

GERMANS TAKE A TRIP

During the latter part of the war, the sporting programme was more and more in the limelight. In fact, it formed a big part of all training arrangements, so much so that each man had to play some game or go on fatigue. Since the war Germany has taken a leaf from our book and are now out and out adherents of physical culture. Their prisoners of war often watched our men down around the base camp. Did that idea come from here?

WOODCUTTERS

WORK FOR HORSES

— DRAWN FROM LIFE. —

FOR G-'S SAKE PULL — HELP! HELP!

MISSED BY INCHES

EXCITING MOMENTS IN THAT FRENCH FOREST AT BONNEVILLE

CUTTING TREES.

WHAT IN THE NAME OF ALL THE SAINTS WILL WE BE AT NEXT?

HOME TO CAMP.

ALL BY —
JIM. MAULTSAID
FRANCE. 1915

Snow was falling as we set out for the woods. Saws, axes, ropes etc., all complete for a new task. It was a white world and looked like Christmas time. Jokes were bandied about: a wag said 'we were going to cut down Christmas trees for the wains' (this is an Ulster one).

A stiff route march brought us to the scene of operations. Trees were marked out for us and the fun then commenced. We knew nothing about this game, but made a start. I never laughed as much in my life. To see a lad up a tree cutting through a branch forgetting all about the weight of his own precious body, then a terrible swish, down came the cutter, saw and branch. Then the language was sweet. Big trees, fair-sized ones and saplings all came under our winning ways. Many a king of the forest we laid low.

FUN WAS GOOD – BUT SORE JOINTS
Good sport no doubt, but we soon found out it was tough heavy work. The hands blistered, our arms got stiff and the back felt like breaking in two. For all that, it kept the blood warm and that was something on a winter's day.

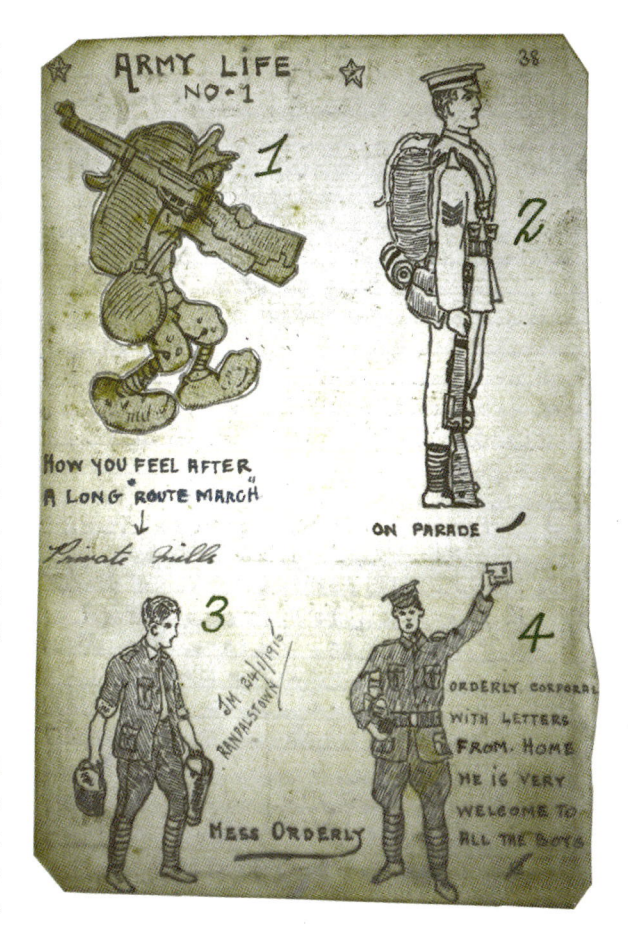

One youth I remember was up some twenty feet or so attaching a hook to a big branch half cut through. He had the rope round once when he slipped, but Lord preserve us, that old hook caught in his coat tails and there he was left 'swinging in the air'.

We laughed until the tears ran down our cheeks. In fact it took quite a time to rescue him. There was no hurry, so the funny man of the squad said, and the words that unfortunate youth used would have done credit to a sergeant-major. No more up the tree for him. He was finished and frightened.

I LOVED THE FOREST
I loved the trees and forests and look back on these few days amongst them and often hoped for the same 'fatigue' but never; it did not fall to my lot again.

WORK FOR HORSES

After cutting down we had to rope them, then all hands on deck for a long strong pull to a clearing and a pile. They were used for dug-out props, gun emplacements, all other requirements.

Cavaliers anglais en reconnaissance | English cavaliers reconnoitring

A WISE OFFICER COMMANDING

Strange work for soldiers! Yes! No doubt, but far better than kicking around cold, miserable billets, trying to keep warm and not succeeding. Our officer commanding was a wise man and, from me anyhow, was appreciated.

THE SUICIDE CLUB

Ordered to a bombing school for the finish of instruction in this art and the chance to secure a badge of merit as a first-class bomber and instructor found me in.

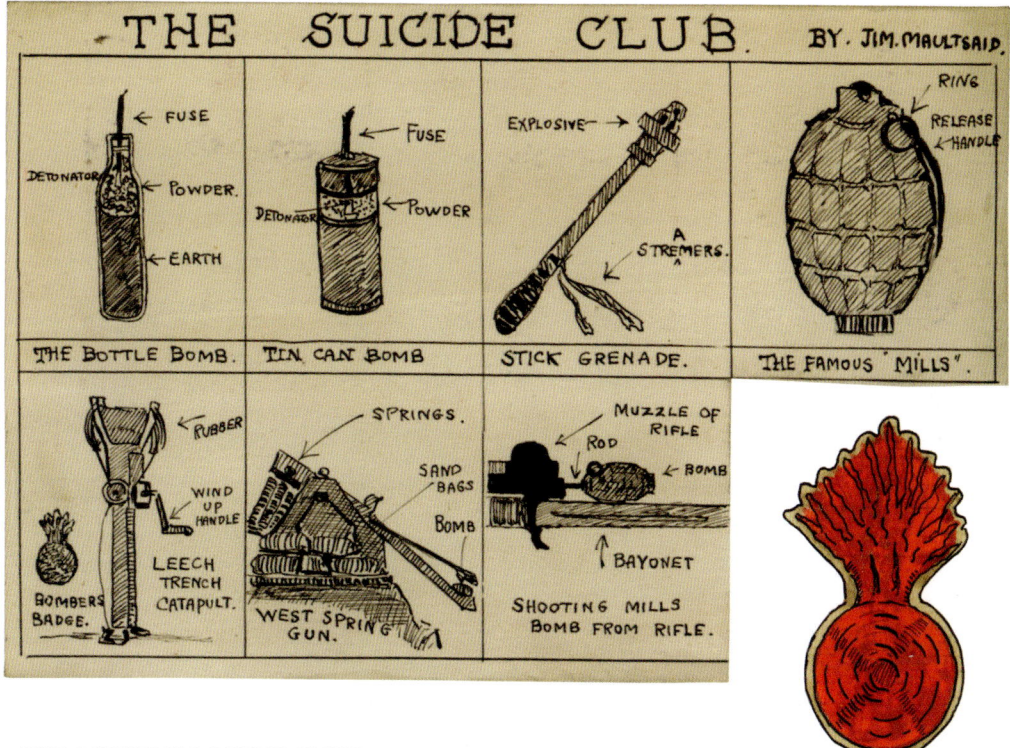

THE GATHERING OF THE CLANS

Here we gathered NCOs from all the 36th Division units all on the same errand. How we worked (at least I did) from morn till night. Lectures and demonstrations every day.

To make, to take down, to throw, to shoot from a rifle (this was a new trick) to act in trenches, how to barricade a trench and how to attack, how to carry and maintain a supply of bombs during attack, we went through it all.

REAL STUFF

Real live stuff was thrown about, just like stones. We blew up dug-outs, we banged at dummies and hurled them from pits into trenches. I enjoyed it fine as the practice was 'IT' and no make believe about the business.

WONDERFUL THROWERS

Some wonderful throwers here. Of course, as a famous general once said, 'If they cannot find bombers in Ireland' where else would you get them? I passed first-class and got my badge.

FROZEN STIFF

Freezing hard all day we had marched at a sharp pace and it was agreeable when the blood warmed up. The night came on and our halting place was a very small village, far too small for a full battalion of one thousand men or so, not to mention our transport.

IN A STRANGE WHITE WORLD AS WE TRUDGED ALONG.

SCRAMBLE FOR SPACE

There was a scramble for space, space that was not to be had. When my section was all fixed up [I had] no place to sleep. High and low I searched. No luck, so giving it up I selected a spot with three walls only, no roof and practically open to the elements. Dog tired, I wrapped the blankets all around myself (after clearing a corner from snow and ice) and lying down I fell asleep – slept well and soundly.

ONLY MY BRAIN WOULD MOVE

Never in all my life have I felt such a feeling. In the early hours my eyes opened and I knew there was something wrong with my body. It was fairly clear and I made an effort to rise. Lord! I could not move hand or foot. Stiff as a board, only my brain was active. All the rest was 'dead'. What a fix! I set up a call for help (thank heavens my tongue was not affected) and in a short time several of my section came hurrying out.

SHOOTING PAINS

They worked with me for over an hour, rubbing snow, grease and massage, until the blood began to shoot through my arms and legs. What agony! Hot drinks of tea from the cookhouse got me on my feet and, Glory be, I was kind of a way ready to 'fall in' and march off with the boys. What a scare it was! It will give you some idea of the intense frost when I tell you that the water in my water bottle was frozen into ice, and this bottle was tightly corked. What a night! One that will live life-long in my memory.

CAREFUL AGAIN

I was careful of the freezing days and nights afterwards; in fact I often spent part of these nights moving about as much as possible.

NO ILL EFFECTS

During that day all ill effects wore off and I was 'right as rain' once more, no fingers or toes lost.

BUILDING HOUSES

Or the house that 'Tommy' built.

No one could describe the looks on the faces of Rogers, Black, or Lewis as I read out the order –

'No. 14 Platoon will parade at 9.00am tomorrow morning for house building.' 'Say Corporal, are you fooling?' 'No my son! Tools will be issued at QM's store, then get stuck into it. Get me?'

RUSH FOR JOBS AS CARPENTERS
True enough, the job was repairing and rebuilding tumbled-down French outhouses and big barns. It was pretty hopeless in some cases, but for all that some marvellous pieces of work were put in and great pride taken by the carpenters, the brick (or stone) masons and plasterers. The plaster was good strong black mud. Most of the cute gents in my little lot rushed the saw and hammer department (it was a cleaner job you see) and [it was] nice to get hammering in big nails.

Walls were rebuilt with raw green pieces of trees, wired in and lathed with smaller bits, then our good cement was splashed on. Holes the size of – well big enough to let a horse and cart through – were fixed up. It was rough and ready work, no doubt, but effective, and what's more was interesting. Far, far better fun than parades or route marching.

Young Lewis, a mere kid no more than fifteen I should say, went up a ladder, when, to our horror, ladder and all came tumbling down. No one hurt, but he lost his job and was put on carrying buckets of cement.

INCINERATORS & LATRINES
Incinerators, latrines etc. were all built also. My section were on the housing scheme, so we knew little of this except from information later.

'PORKY' GETS A BUMP
'Porky' Black got struck on the head with a falling beam. When he came to, he wanted to murder the guilty ones. We held him back.

'DADDY' TAKES THE HUFF
'Daddy' McBride took charge of a wall. That was a stiff proposition and after a whole morning's work the d*** thing fell in with a crash like a bursting shell. Cheers went up as 'Dad' was a 'know-all' and a bit on the aggressive side, so it gave great satisfaction to some of the troops. He took the huff, told us to bury the b ***** thing ourselves and took little or any part in further operations. The wall was 'demobbed'.

I DON'T WANT TO GO TO THE TRENCHES NO MORE (SO SAID THE SONG)

How many of the 'boys' who served in the Great War can't bring to mind this old song? Very few I'm sure.

'DEE STREET' IN FRANCE
Want it or not, here we are after some wandering around, looking over no man's land once more. A new sector to us, but it seems quite homely seeing such names as 'Donegall Pass', 'Dee Street', 'Newtownards Road', 'Broadway Avenue', etc. on the signboards. No mistake here, it's a Belfast lot we have relieved, and it was.

WHAT ARE THEY DOING AT HOME?
The weather was – well, it was dead of winter – and snow, ice, frost and rain all had a spell in their own sweet way. Conditions were deplorable, overhead and underfoot. One of the most awful 'spells' I ever put in, in a line.

My little book tells me it was a Saturday we took over on, and my thoughts have turned to 'home'. 3.00pm. The Blues would be kicking off at this minute. Funny thoughts! What? But then we often turned our minds 'homewards' on things our loved ones would be doing, just at this minute. Would we ever get the chance to do it ourselves?

RUIN EVERYWHERE
All the villages on our way in were in ruins. 'Jerry' played his big guns on them every day – looking for our reserves I suppose. Quite a 'hot spot' this, and lots of excitement.

CRASH! All THE EARTH FALLS IN
Crash! Darkness and trembling earth. What's wrong? I was smashed up against a wooden post and half stunned. Then the roof of our little dug-out fell in on top of us, five or six living souls. A shell had hit it, a bull's-eye, and got us. 'Are you hurt, Corporal?' 'No I don't think so! Are you?' 'No! … but we are gasping for breath.' Not a sign of daylight either, and that awful clay was choking our life away. Quick boys! Great good fortune had it: a spade in the dug-out. Good!

Never did I work like this. Turn about as our breath failed, and it was failing fast, would we be all smothered? What a death, like rats, but, No! No! No! A gleam of daylight. Hurry man, hurry. Bigger and bigger the hole got and I emerged, free, into God's pure air.

Never did I take such a lung opener. It was sweet. One by one we helped each other out, pleased and happy – all safe. Shaken up in all our bones, but not one wounded. A narrow call, and this all on the good Lord's day too!

HOW WE SUFFERED
Sleet and rain now! How we suffered. No one knows the misery of cold, cold feet, useless hands almost, and a 'want' in the very pit of one's stomach – no one knows unless they came through it.

THE GUNS
The guns? There was so much more activity at this time, especially from the other side. Have we no shells at all?

ROCKETS IN HUNDRED
Enemy rockets lit up the sky at night. It was a sight to see them soar away up into the sky, then burst, hang over for a few seconds and fade into the blackness of the night. Supplies were plentiful 'over there' as it was an all-night 'show', every night.

TWO LONE SCOUTS
'Jim! Will you come out with me tonight?' Lieutenant Wedgewood was at my elbow. 'Yes sir! What time do I report to you?' 'About 12.00pm will do.' The little dug-out witnessed a change as buckles, buttons and faces are all blacked over. Big six-shooters are strapped on, a Mills bomb into each pocket and we splash out, passing our sentries, who stand like shadows. A whispered password and the order to pass along that we had gone out – then up over the top and in amongst our own wire. This ground had all been carefully 'spotted out' by us during the daytime and plans laid.

SOME POOR SOUL?
Carefully we moved. It was slow work (as always). A false step and, splash! you were into an evil-smelling shell-hole. What a smell hereabouts. Some poor soul's body was going the way of all flesh.

WE ARE PARTED
Side by side we slide along, sometimes on our full 'stretch out' and at others on hands and knees. Oh! It was dark! And cold sleet blowing. A bad night. Star shells and rockets stilled our hearts, turning us into statues on the spot. Gradually across the damp ground, the long dank grass wetting us through, we made our way. Turning to nudge Mr Wedgewood I was surprised to find him missing. My heart stopped beating. Where was he? Not a sign anywhere – and it was as black as it could be. Then it was blowing a hurricane and the snow was on; where was my friend? In the name of the saints what had happened to him? Around and around I crawled for almost an hour but never a word or trace of him. Had he gone back without me? Somehow I felt and knew he was safe.

LOST! NO! YES!
Making up my mind to return I then retraced my steps, but had a feeling I was on the wrong track.

On and on I went! But where? Lost? Slowly the thought dawned on me that I was out here all on my own and 'lost'. Visions of being a prisoner of war floated through my mind. Not that! Not that! Steady yourself, Jim, your nerves are going. My body was now all cold and panic seized me, but just for a minute or so.

SCOUT CRAFT TO MY HELP

All my years of scout craft came to my help and, knowing that a person lost in the dark always goes round in circles, I tried to work out my turnings. Then, judging the star shells, I picked out the enemy line, turned about and walked, yes just staggered, straight up (didn't crawl) in the direction of our lines. The wire was thick; I cut myself, pants and puttees were torn, but slowly I wormed my way in. Was I right? God! My breath now came in gasps. Not a sound from the fire-step as I appeared over the crest. Taking my courage in both hands I slid over and in.

HANDS UP

Hands up! We have you! And they had me. But the voice was Irish. A listening post of five had been following my movements for the past fifteen minutes on the alert! Yes! That was a smart lot. Explanations followed. I was a mile or so from the 14th Rifles; this was the trenches of one of our lots but not my own.

I collapsed from exposure and cold.

Kind friends led me (or carried, I do not know) back to the reserve line. An old cellar, a big brazier, all my clothes were taken off. Hot tea pushed into me and then, wrapped in several blankets, I soon recovered.

RE-UNION – OLD FRIENDS

Thanking my rescuers, I was now anxious to get back to my own battalion and straightaway in the early hours of the morning set out as I did not want to be posted as 'missing'.

The reunion with Mr Wedgewood was a glad affair. Oh! he was pleased, and so was yours truly, Jim Maultsaid.

AFTERTHOUGHTS

Footnote. We lost scores of men from frostbite during this turn in the line; 'French feet' it was called but, thank goodness, I missed this misfortune. Tins of some evil-smelling grease were issued. This stuff had to be faithfully rubbed in each night. The troops did not take too kindly as it seemed to make the feet colder than ever, but I suppose it was for our own good, like the tot of rum issued each morning. This tot never went down my throat as I would not take it. For all that, let me say: many a life it saved.

NOT FORGOTTEN

<u>By the boys in green and black</u>

Up to this time our Battalion had had their fair share of casualties and it was with regret that we 'missed' a pal from the ranks. Going in with him to the line and then having to take his name from the list with the big black score 'Dead' – well it brought a lump to your throat. Sad to see them go, but it was God's will and we could not ordain it otherwise. The worst part was when 'his' letters arrived and he, poor lad, – gone forever. Patrick McGill's old lines come to mind:

> On the March, in the trench,
> I can see you still
> Mate of the old platoon.

JOURNEY'S END

As we stood aside to let Sergeant Hunter or the MO (stretcher bearers' branch) pass out down the communication trench with a sad burden for a little grave that night in a quiet spot, or some little French graveyard, well – it brought a tear to your eyes and we saluted, yet somehow I often thought 'it's nice to die like that – in the prime of youth … and not grow old, as we do'.

SACRED THOUGHTS

I do not intend hammering your feelings as most stories do by describing how these boys died; that's something we old soldiers keep to ourselves and these thoughts are sacred – at least to me they are.

NAMES THAT LIVE

I can bring to mind only a few of the names of our first early casualties, Sergeant Penman, Sergeant Stevenson, Private Lorimer, etc., etc., etc., etc.

AND WE MARCH ON …

These boys will long be remembered by all of us and are on our Roll of Honour, gone forever from this earth but 'Not Forgotten'.

Gone to answer the Reveille up above, leaving a blank in the ranks below. Such is a soldier's life.

By the right – quick march – and we

MARCH ON.

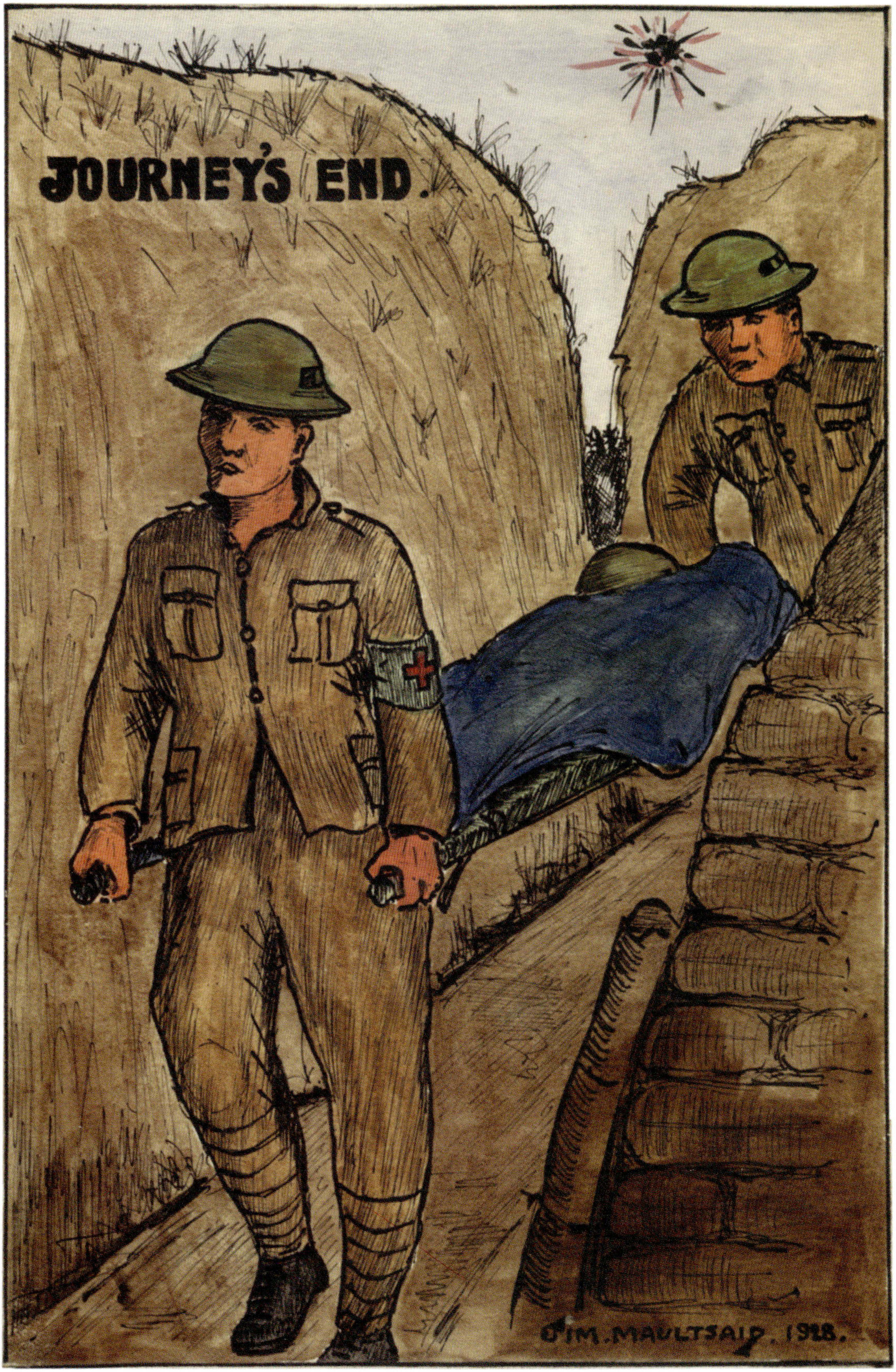
JOURNEY'S END.
JIM. MAULTSAID. 1928.

IN RESERVE

D COMPANY WILL HOLD THE RESERVE LINE
On the face of it this looked a 'soft tack', but was not the 'gift' we half expected. A change for us, for all that, and my duties were far different to the front-line stuff.

WORKING PARTIES – DAY AND NIGHT
We were only five or six hundred yards from the firing line, just close enough in case of trouble, but most of our trouble came from the back in the shape of orders for 'trench repairs', 'working parties', 'ration and rum parties', in fact, all kinds of 'parties'.

HARD TO FORGET
Some never-to-be-forgotten 'comic' and otherwise incidents came our way during this spell on 'reserve'.

BANG GOES THE DIXIE AND OUR DINNER
One fine day we were all crowding around our dixie that had just arrived with hot stew when the very sky seemed to open and fall on the parapet of the trench we were all standing at. Thrown in all directions in the mud, up went 'stew', mess orderlies and us, to pick ourselves up shaken and scared to find 'all lost'.

No dinner that day for my little squad.

AND THE RUM
It's pitch dark, the trench is eighteen inches deep in water and mud. Progress is slow. We decide to get up and walk on ground alongside. The two boys with a pail and two jars of rum are in my special care as this was a precious cargo. Getting along in fine style when rat – ta – tat – tat – like a hammer goes Jerry's machine gun. Down we go – flat as a pancake. The gun sweeps round and we gather ourselves and cargo. Horror! Of horrors! Can you credit it – both jars are – 'napoo', smashed [napoo: from the French il n'ay en a plus: there's no more].

This was a fine fix now. Nothing could be done so we plied on, but our story cut little ice when 'no rum' was forthcoming. The looks should have killed me and my squad. I personally in my heart did not regard it as a great loss, but others did.

JAM – BULLY – AND – WIRE.

A SURE STARTER "BULLY"

~ALWAYS WITH US~

"Daddy McBride sees the Jam." — Jim Maultsaid 1916

JAM — Plum & Apple

"WIRE WORK" — Simply wrapped up in this subject

BANG GOES THE RUM JARS

IN RESERVE IT WAS A GIFT!

WIRE

WHERE DID THAT ONE GO?

OH! LORD — Plum & Apple

RATIONS

TWO OLD RELIABLES 'JAM AND BULLY'
'Twelve tins of jam. Twelve of bully. Yes! That completes your lot, Corporal. Go ahead. Wait a moment – here's six rolls of barbed wire for C Company.' (A voice from the back, 'To hell with C Company and the wire.')

'Keep quiet there!'

JAM AND BULLY BEEF
Don't mention them! We lived on them. When short of sugar for your tea – use jam! When short of milk for your porridge – use jam! In fact, my good housewife, if you are ever stuck – use jam!

Also, as for 'bully', you can put it to a hundred uses. For example – you can make 'stew' from it in ninety-nine different ways. Just mention it to any 'old sweat'!!!!!!!

X'MAS DAY 1915

LUCK was on our side and we were clear for a short spell from all the worries and cares of 'up there' when Christmas Day 1915 dawned.

WE CALLED HER MOTHER
The dawn was wet, cold and miserable. I had struck one of the best rest billets that ever fell my way. In fact it was the parlour of a neat little home and the only occupant was a silver-haired old lady. She was a real 'gem' and no error. Nothing would do but we would leave the old loft and take her best room.

Now this was a treat for us and we kept it in lovely condition. Big dirty feet were well cleaned before entering (mind you she laid down no laws and this pleased us). No restrictions and we took no liberties. At night it was her delight to get us all gathered round (about twelve of us) and lay out a neat little supper. My, she was simply adorable. We all loved her so.

JUST A LITTLE PRESENT
Came Christmas morn, as I said before, and my first duty was to hand 'mother' as we called her a Christmas gift from the boys of a fifty-franc note. No! No! She could not take it and the tears streamed down her cheeks. In my best French I tried to explain that it would offend my squad if she did not accept. 'Ah! Bon, Irish soldiers.'

FROM THE IRISH BOYS
Much coaxing, at last she agreed and took it. Never was a gift more heartily given.

WE GET JOLLY
Sports in the morning. Plum pudding at dinner hour. I remember it was 'sticky stuff' and hard to digest, so my share was light. We washed it down with 'vin-blong' and 'citron' (this is not good French or English either), but it's what we called them and will do very well. Night falls. We have sing-songs. Stories about the past. Ghosts as per usual. More wine [but] 'not for me, a strict old TT'.

SEE STORY
X'MAS DAY. 1915

"WE CALLED HER MOTHER"

The boys get very jolly.

Well! Well! Let them. God alone knows how many of us will be together for Christmas 1916.

Somehow or other, I did not feel too happy as I kept on thinking – thinking – thinking.

RING-A-ROSES

Mother sits in the corner, beaming on us all. Never a word of reproach for all the noise and uproar. What a din!

GOODNIGHT – 'BON SWAR'

Now boys, time for bed! And Christmas day was over once more. Like children we put our mother in the middle of the floor, danced round ring–a–ring–a–roses style and sang for 'she's a jolly good fellow', then to sleep. She tucked quite a few of them in and whispered 'Bon swar, my cherries', and I replied 'God bless you'.

ON THE TRAMP

NO rest for the wicked – 'well we must have sinned a lot.'

Blast that band! Dry up for goodness sake! Drown it! Pity the poor band, and they, poor fellows, blowing their lungs out for us – yes! all for us – and this is how the famous D Company is talking now. Our trouble was – we were at least two hundred yards from the band – sound does not travel like a flash of light – so when the music reached our ears, it was out of tune and we were put out of step, a bad business when feet are like lead and the old pack like a two hundredweight, and the strap cutting the flesh to the bone. For all that, many's a weary mile they helped us to cover – and forget our troubles too. God bless Regimental Sergeant Major Elphic. He was proud of his band.

BATTERED FROM PILLAR TO POST

From town to town we were battered. Here tonight, gone in the morning. It was move – halt – move again. New scenery, new sites, new billets (when we got any) and ever on – we marched.

Our sins must have been legion!

KID LEWIS KNOCKED OUT!

Halt! Your billet is in that house, in the loft. Through to it by the kitchen. A sour-faced old dame stands in the doorway. Pardon me, Madame, we must get in! I had to brush her aside and her face was far from pleasant. Up goes the section, up a narrow stairway. All up but one, young Lewis. Halfway there I hear a crash and down comes a shower of water and a broken bottle.

That old dame flew up those stairs. I flew after her. She had poor 'Kid' Lewis by the hair and was battering him unmercifully. I grasped her, not very gently, and threw her off. She turned on me; it took several of us to hold and subdue her and push her down the stairs. She was screaming! What a reception to a new home! What did that precious bottle

THE INCINERATOR.

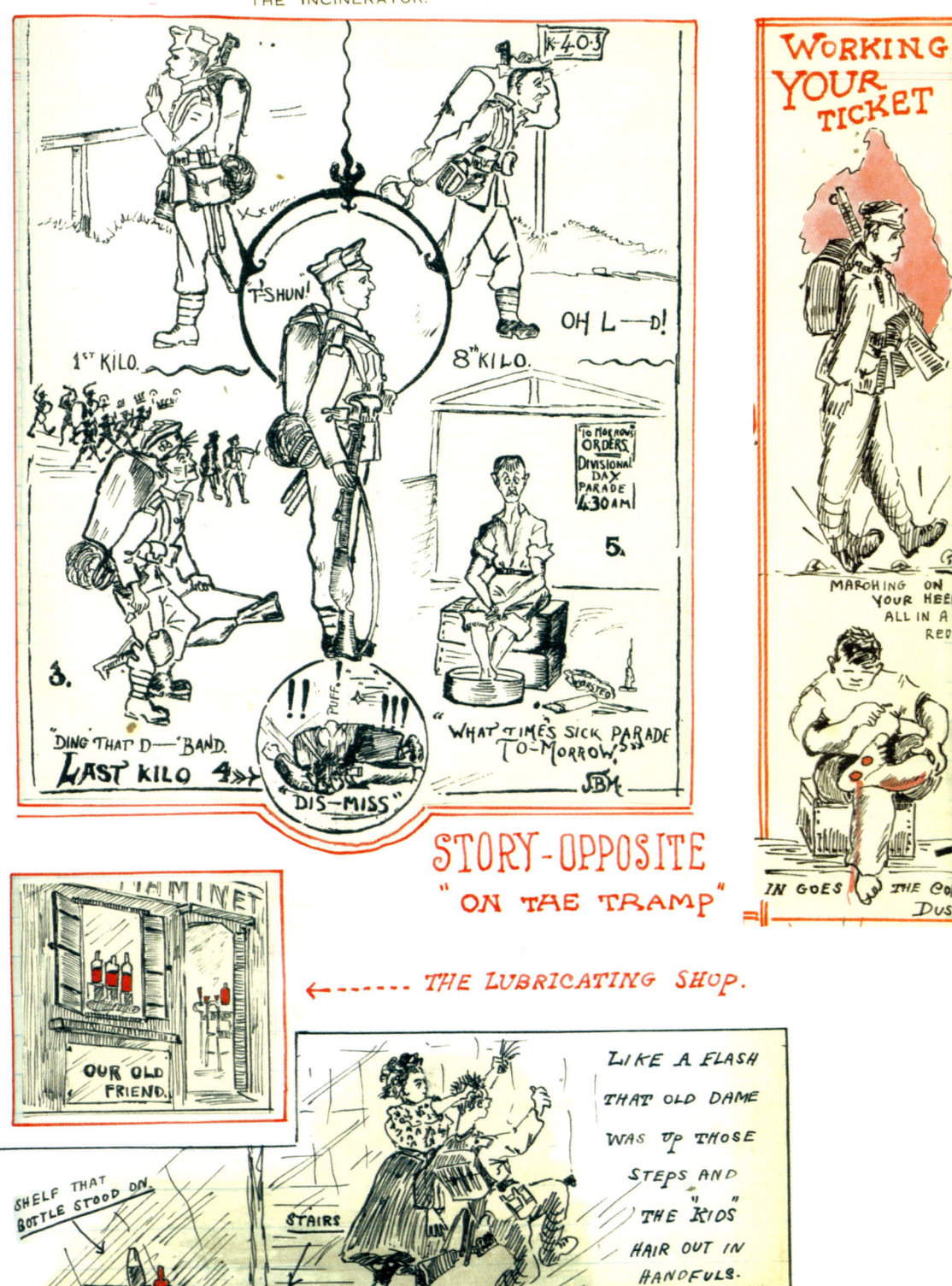

contain? I don't know, but suspected it was holy water. I threatened to report her to my company commander and she calmed down.

From this until we left several days later she could not have been nicer, but the 'Kid' was scared and kept clear of the kitchen as much as possible. We gave her the 'bird', that is to say nothing was bought in her shop, or no jobs (for payment), so we had our revenge.

SOUVENIR
On the day of departure she was handed a five-franc note and she slipped me a 'tiny bottle of water'. Souvenir! I kept it for many months.

WORKING YOUR TICKET

[Illustrations with captions: "THE SUFFERINGS OF A SOAP EATER", "AFTER A DOSE OF CORDITE", "ONE THROUGH THE FOOT.", "ALL PICTURES BY JIM.MAULTSAID"]

How it was done
　Some cute moves were tried I know by a few (very few) of the troops to 'get out of it' and have a spell in 'Blighty'.

THE OLD TRICKS
One was eating soap. Another was to take the lead out of a bullet and get the cordite; this was also eaten. Of course, the most common was a nice bullet through the arm, leg or foot, the shot being fired by the 'hero' himself. All these were common property and the medical people were well up to these dodges.

AND A NEW ONE

But here goes a true story of how it was worked and well worked too. Sandy G ---, one of my lot, a poor soldier I may say, a grouse, in fact 'a no user' longed for his 'ticket' and got it. His brain worked out the following: every soldier knows that after a scorching route march he has one or two bad blisters. Well, Sandy opened one of these, then scraped a copper coin (a penny or half-penny) and dropped the dust into the blister.

Ye gods! What a leg and foot. Rank poison. Went up like a balloon. Did he lose the leg? I cannot say!

KNIFE THROWERS

Hearing strange sounds woke me up very, very early in a little village we were lying in. I had the feeling that something was wrong and, getting up hurriedly, threw on a few bits of clothing, then ventured forth. After a few minutes I located the hubbub. Peering through a crack in a tumbledown courtyard I was astounded to see a party of coloured troops prancing around, each with a long knife in his hand. What was the game? These were Indian troops, Gurkhas, I think, but I'm not quite sure. Anyhow, one took a short race and a knife flashed through the air straight as a bullet to sink into the wooden door some twenty yards away; each of the others followed suit, then a rush was made to the target to examine the shooting and the 'target' was a 'live' one, but not a hair on his head had even been touched, so far as I can see. It was all for a gamble, I think, or some form of competition. Pity the Germans in the hand-to-hand battle with this lot.

FRENCH OR BRITISH
I COULD NOT SAY

FRENCH BEAUTIES ?

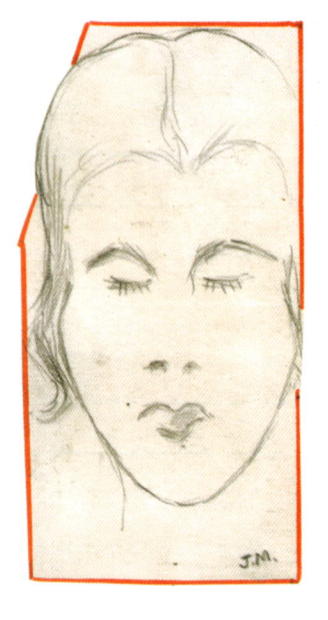

'MADAMOISELLE'

YOU can take it from me that the troops (by troops, I mean the real 'storm battalions', not the 'base wallopers') did not get much chance to 'parley–vous' with 'Mademoiselle' of France.

WHAT THEY LOOKED LIKE TO ME

Of course we did, now and again, see the real French lassies on our travels and my idea of their charms you have an opportunity of judging for yourself. Can they beat ours? I don't think so! The sketches are all from life but, of course, the subject did not sit for me; it was 'my impressions' taken by the brain photographic box, then, first chance in the billet, I put them on paper. The only one that gave me a few minutes to get the outline was the full length picture, and this costume was worn only for the day I think; it was some national festival or other and too good for me to miss. So there you are! Charming, no doubt, in many ways. I knew of no 'romances'.

A HEN THAT 'WESTWARD' WENT

SERG – ON, SERG – ON, CORPORAL – CORPORAL

Quite an uproar outside our billet. The sergeant was not available (as usual) so I 'lit in for it'.
    'What's wrong now?' What the h★★★ is ever right – out here?
    'Wee, wee' Madame (Yes! Yes) and, my, she was in some rage! Did I see her, what? For the love of Mike, speak English. No, I did not see it! And I turned to move into the 'rest'

THE HEN THAT WESTWARD WENT.

again. She grabbed me, this hardened mother of France, and led me to the hen run. Ah! I see now – you are short a hen, and it's a big fat one. Your 'soldiers' took it, pointing to my famous platoon's headquarters. No! No! Madame.

But she maintained they did and they would have to pay for it and the price asked I am sure five times too much.

NO TRACE
No trace! No one knew anything about hens. in fact I hadn't noticed even one in around these parts. Of course not.

DAILY INTERVIEWS
Day and daily for a solid week I was interviewed about this 'bird', still missing; but I am moving too fast.

REAL SOUP
That night I got something in the lid of my dixie that was real and truly soup and d*** good stuff too.

ENLIGHTENMENT
We said goodbye, moved on, and that hen, that 'Westward went', never, never in this world would grace that old farmyard. Many months later the story was unfolded to me as per above sketch, but madame was slipped a ten-franc note for 'damages' before we departed.

THE LISTENING POST

Running out in front of fire trench these little posts or 'saps' were very important, and one or two, and sometimes three, men were put out as an advance guard or screen to the main line. It was usually a narrow little bit of a trench and ended about the edge of our wire. Duty on these posts was special stuff, the utmost quietness was maintained, eyes and ears strained for several hours to catch the slightest sound or movement by the enemy.

Communication to the front line was usually a long cord or wire with a bell or several jam tins tied on. Pulling this was to bring the troops to 'the alert'. Having to lie quite flat (in the mud if necessary) was not uncommon, just a sandbag or two as protection. Last spell in the line demanded a lot of this unpleasant work. It was a nerve-racking week, but I pulled through.

A FRENCH IDEA
Snipers posts' crackshots had this job. A certain spot on *the* enemy line was picked out, the rifle trained on it and set (fixed), then the slightest move and 'crack' went the sniper's rifle. Jerry's sharpshooters were very unpopular; he always seemed to lay a lead on our latrines. A very ancient device was picked up by us and it appeared to be a French tip. A frame of wood for five rifles to sit on (fixed), a cord ran through the triggers, then one pull and bang went five shots. See pictures opposite page.

Star Shell Reflections 1914–1916

THE OLD AND THE NEW

IN 1914-1918.

THE TANKS 1915-16-17-18 REPRESENTED THE ELEPHANTS?

INTO ACTION.

THREW BOMBS HUNDREDS OF YEARS AGO.

HAND-TO-HAND IN THE GREAT WAR.

WE TRIED THIS IN 1915-16 CATAPULT GUN

EVEN THESE WERE "KILLED"

This photograph, sent by a *Daily Sketch* reader, shows a battered tank on the Menin road in 1918.

ALMOST BACK TO THE BOW & ARROW?

SOMETHING NEW.

PONTOON BRIDGES.

TRUMPETS THOUSANDS OF YEARS AGO.

THE ATTACK MODERN STYLE.

BUGLES STILL.

SOME COMPARISONS

It was written before the Great War that armies would never again meet in hand-to-hand combat. Shows you what the experts knew? With all the modern use of steel, gas, tanks etc., there is no getting away from it, the infantryman had to finish the job, and I suppose it will be the same again (not in our generation, I hope). Study the previous five pages and note the similarity of some methods, thousands of years old and, yet, *new*? I try to give you several examples of how the ancients were copied during 1914-1918. The elephant and the tank. How does that go? The bow and arrow. Well! We shot over bombs by springs. War chariots. What about our field artillery and six chargers going into action? Bombs! They were throwing them hundreds of years ago. Battle flags carried by some regiments, but not into battle, except on rare occasions when individuals took some battalion sign or motto over the top. You can read about the triumphs of war in the Bible, we had our bands and our bugles too! Horses have figured in history of battle right down the ages. They figured again in the last big war, but are now doomed, I'm afraid, for ever. The aeroplane was new and the wireless and the …

CRAWLING BACK

HERE goes a little confession. A winter's night, dark, wet, and of course the mud.

LEGS GIVE UP

Our lot have been relieved from front-line duty. We reach the end of a long communication trench and reach a road (hard surface). What's wrong with my legs and feet? I stagger and slide down. The rifle acts as a walking stick. It's no use. I cannot stand up. I have lost the power in my legs from the trunk down. 'Say, Rogers, can you stand?' 'No! Corporal I'm 'all up'.' 'Hell! What will we do? Many of the boys like this?' 'Yes, quite a few. Move on there, from the rear.' We cannot move on, so crawl to the ditch and lie until our chums passed by. Ashamed of ourselves, but there you are, not a move in us. Funny, the body is all right! Here go my lads, I'm 'crawling back'. Yes, we crawled all the way up an old muddy shell-torn road on our hands and knees for more than two miles. The spirit to win here! And win we did. Broken and bleeding.

CRAWLING BACK.

BY. JIM. MAULTSAID.

THE RIFLE ACTS AS A WALKING STICK

ANY DUFF SAM?

Sam was a cook, that is to say an army cook. I would not care to say he had been one in civilian life; if so he would have been out of work pretty often I'm afraid.

WHAT DUFF WAS
Now 'duff' was a kind of pudding and that was Sam's strong point, the making of it. At least he said so, but joking apart it was not bad stuff.

UNPRINTABLE

His reply to your question of 'any duff, Sam?' is unprintable. Suffice to say it annoyed him 'sore', the asking this question; why I don't know, but it did.

DROOPING MOUSTACHE

Sam was tall and thin, possessed a pair of long drooping moustaches that he often stroked thoughtfully. Catch him in this mood and your luck was in – you had an extra helping – and perhaps you did not.

JUST AS BLACK

To see him ambling along after his black 'cooker cart', just shuffling along was a sight, and I hardly ever remember seeing him any cleaner looking than his cart, and it was jet black. This was a byword amongst the troops and so long as a 14th Rifles man lives the password is ******.

DO YOU REMEMBER?

HOW … we looked for the postman? No mail, the old heart sank. No word from home? A parcel and a letter or two, and the – a new world for us.

THE … old French man and his funny barrow? He worked from morn till night. We often gave a hand in the barn and earned his goodwill. Good business.

DID … you forget the 'Wells'? Water was as precious as gold. The pumps were often locked against us. Quite a few of our boys remember them; they were down.

YES … and the cheese! All colours, green, yellow, and black. Some of it could have gone on the march by itself, if we had not eaten it up.

WHEN … we had no billets and had to make little bivouacs from the ground sheets and old bags? Back to Adam's day, and sometimes not even a bivouac.

AND … the cigarettes we got? Fairy Queen, Golden Nimrod, Black Jack, Shining Jewel, etc., etc. Coffin nails every one. Fortunes from the troops.

CIGARETTES! THE PACKET WAS BEST PART.

YET … with it all, can't you remember the share-and-share alike spirit? A treasure to live for evermore.

SHOOTING BACKWARDS

He pulled the trigger and – bang! The barrel leaped out from the wood casing and twisted right round like a hoop.

MORNING INSPECTION

At Stand-to each morning it was the custom for the platoon officer to inspect the rifles, after we had finished our five rounds of rapid fire. Now it needed quite a lot of work to clean out our barrels, but a few shots left them nice and bright, just in order for the daily inspection.

BANG! FLASH!

This private had not shot a single shot at Stand-to, then, like a flash, it dawned on him about rifle inspection. Jumping up on the fire-step he let rip when, to our horror, the barrel rose up, turned into the shape of a hoop and he fell down with shock and fright. What the h★★★? Hurriedly, we collected our wits, dumped the offending rifle out into the wire (after examination) and, by good luck, got him another rifle in time for Lieutenant Monard's rounds.

SHOOTING BACKWARDS

Jim Maultsaid.

The cause of it? All quite simple: on the previous day this unfortunate mortal had struck the muzzle of his rifle in the mud, then, during the night, this turned quite solid, like cement. Get me? He pulled the trigger, the bullet travelled up to the hard mud, then, meeting resistance there, had to get out somehow, so it probably burst the barrel. The result is as already described.

A shock and a warning to Private McC★★★. He was careful in future with firearms and never let a speck of dirt or dust even light on his rifle. It was a joke no doubt amongst the boys, but for all that he might have lost a hand or part of his face. A narrow shave.

THE MAD MAJOR

So we called him. Mad or sane he was a brave man, and we, the infantrymen in the trenches marvelled at his daring.

YES! WE KNEW HIM

Early in 1916 we knew him on the Somme. How or where he got his name I cannot say and how we knew it was 'he' in the air is hard to explain, but somehow there was something about his antics that told us that we were right when the cry went up – there he goes, 'the mad major'.

[Illustration: biplane sketch captioned "THE MAD MAJOR. — Just a bundle of bamboo and canvas. He turned and twisted. A pioneer of our famous airmen.? A hero too!" Margin note: "Drawn in front line at Beaumont-Hamel 1916 – J.M."]

HIS WARM RECEPTION

Now the machines we had in 1915–16 were nothing like those of later years, and to see him sail over the German lines in his bamboo and canvas skeleton so low that we could almost see his face as he passed over was to us a marvel. How he escaped death God only knows as the guns, large and small, also rifle fire, that gave him a welcome was 'hot'. When he sailed over we generally let a few shots go at the German front line to assist him as much as possible.

ONE OF THE PIONEERS

He was one of the pioneer airmen and the forerunner of the bravest band of flyers the world has ever known.

REGIMENTAL COLOURS

Each regiment has its own colours. Some of these are very old indeed and have been handed down from generation to generation. They are works of art and usually made of silk, the threads used running into scores of thousands. All battle honours are added on and these often date back hundreds of years. It is the custom in some battalions to teach the recruits about each battle 'his own' battalion took part in and how it was won, especially by the help of his lot. The previous pages should interest you.

REGIMENTAL COLOURS

REGIMENTAL COLOURS

REGIMENTAL COLOURS

THE AIR BOYS

A more devil-may-care lot of men I never met than our air force boys in the Great War.

HOW DID THEY FLY

How some of them got into the air at all in the machines of early days beats me. Like all the other branches of warfare we were sadly outclassed at the very outset, but nearing the end we had the best air force the world has ever known up to that time.

WATCHING THE MACHINES

We often watched with bated breath the hairbreadth escapes of our boys, and how they dared to face the 'black arrows' of our enemy made us marvel, but face and beat them they often did. To see our lone red, white and blue plane amongst several 'black cross' machines pumping lead, ducking, side-stepping, looking like a fly, away up in the blue sky was a treat for us. Dogfights often took place, but we noticed that 'Jerry' always had good high space to work in and came over in relays. He worried us a lot with bombs and we did not fancy them much. The gunfire from the ground did not appear much good in checking the invaders.

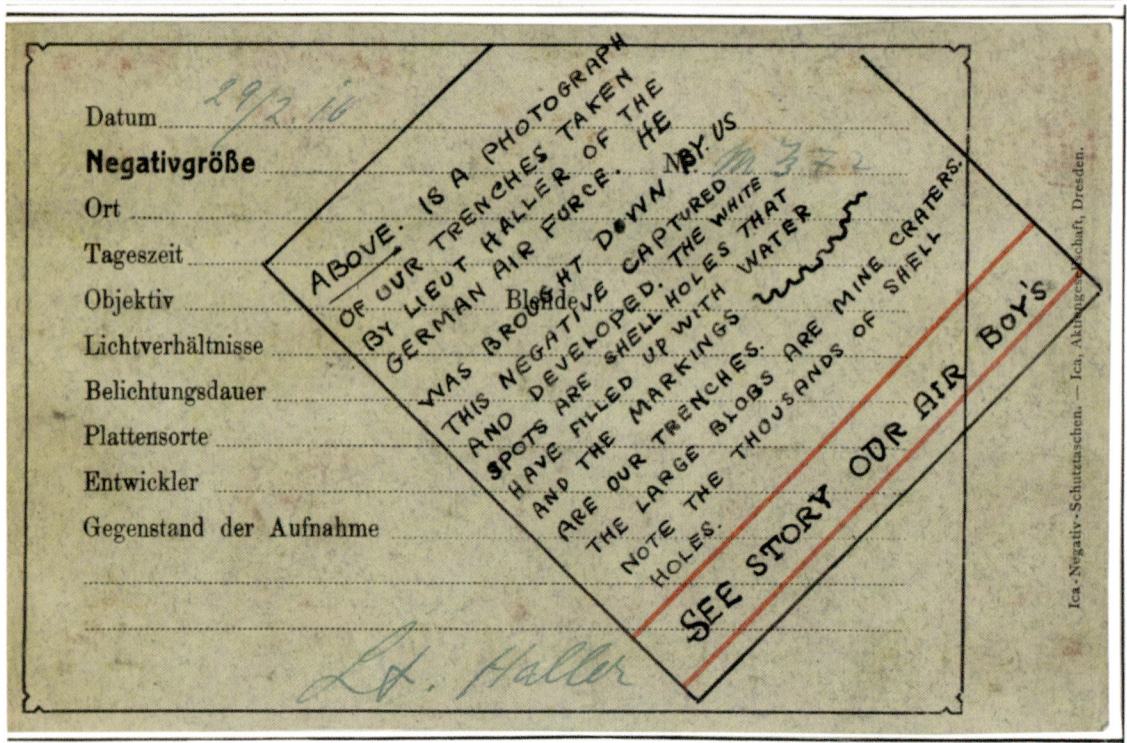

Star Shell Reflections 1914–1916

Datum	29/2.16
Negativgröße	M 372
Ort	
Tageszeit	
Objektiv	
Lichtverhältnisse	
Belichtungsdauer	
Plattensorte	
Entwickler	
Gegenstand der Aufnahme	

ABOVE IS A PHOTOGRAPH OF OUR TRENCHES TAKEN BY LIEUT HALLER OF THE GERMAN AIR FORCE. HE WAS BROUGHT DOWN BY US Beside THIS NEGATIVE CAPTURED AND DEVELOPED. THE WHITE SPOTS ARE SHELL HOLES THAT HAVE FILLED UP WITH WATER AND THE MARKINGS ARE OUR TRENCHES. NOTE THE LARGE BLOBS ARE MINE CRATERS. THE THOUSANDS OF SHELL HOLES.

SEE STORY ODR AIR BOY'S

Lt. Haller

72

OUR AIR BOYS WERE FULL OF "DEVIL".

ONE OF OUR LADS GIVES CHASE

AN AWFUL DEATH! A HUN MACHINE PLUNGING DOWN — ONE WING BURNT OFF

SINGLE COMBAT.

ALL PICTURES TAKEN FROM MY WAR SKETCH BOOK

THE WAR ABOVE US

WE SHUDDER!

JIM. MAULTSAID.

THAT SOMETIMES CAME DOWN TO US

DOWN — DOWN HE SWOOPED!

OUTNUMBERED IN MACHINES BUT — WE HAD —

WE IMPROVED GREATLY IN 1917 — ON OBSERVATION DUTY OVER ENEMY LINES.

SKETCH BY. J.M. FRANCE. 1916.

TYPICAL AIR FORCE OFFICER.

AN ARIEL DOG FIGHT

JIM. MAULTSAID. 1916. FROM MY WAR DIARY

OUR AIR BOYS

THE FINEST AIRMEN OF THE GREAT WORLD WAR

ON THE WIRE

WIRING PARTY

A nice job this! I don't think. Barbed wire in rolls. Stakes of iron and wood. Mallets covered with sandbags and a real dark night. 'All ready boys?' 'Yes!' 'Out you go!' Slipping and sliding, we scrambled over the parapet with our ungainly loads to start work.

Here's the spot (this place had been blown to atoms during the day, leaving about twenty-five yards or so of a gap in our wire defences) and we commence. Big rough gloves are worn to save our poor hands. In goes a stake. Thud! Thud! For G★★★'s sake hit it easy. Each blow sounds like a thunderclap. In goes another stake, then the lads unravel some wire and wrap it around in loops. Flash! What's that? A star shell. We stand like the posts themselves. It dies down. Not a cough, or word spoken. Just thud! thud! Thud! Then zip – zip-zip-ping – p-i-n-g.

Has Jerry spotted us? Terrible this, standing up and the bullets crashing past. Slowly we complete our task and get the order to 'come in'. You don't breathe easily until your body slides back into the trench again.

'HARD TACK'

It is recorded in my little book that in early 1916, during a spell in line, that we were reduced to the 'hard tack' (Army biscuits). White bread was scarce, so scarce in fact that it disappeared from our daily diet.

GOOD FOR DENTIST

Now these 'teeth smashers' were never too popular, yet, with nothing else available, they filled up the blank spaces in the lower regions.

LABELS SAID 'HARD-DRY'

Hard – dry on the box – they were all that! Do you ever imagine making porridge from biscuits? Some milk (tinned stuff) some sugar (or jam), two or three of the above in the dixie lid, brought to the boil and, lo!, it was 'Irish stew porridge' when cool.

10d - A SLICE FOR BREAD

Or dip them in your tea to soften them. Not a bad move. How did sailors live on these all the time? Not so bad now and again, but try a steady week's work on them, and you never forget'em. No, never! Day and daily, they turn up. In the stew, in the tea, and in the supper menu. Oh! Boy! A franc for a slice of bread (from home) was offered, and a franc then was 10d [less than 5p]. Biscuits – hard – dry – enough! Enough!

Star Shell Reflections 1914–1916

YES - - - SERGEANT

Slandered and often vowed vengeance against, the poor sergeant had a lot to put up with. Of course, he never heard half of it (or a quarter), so it did not hurt so much. There were all kinds of these fellows. Good, bad and indifferent. By indifferent, I don't mean to the sufferings of the privates. Ah! Dear no! They knew all that, having been at one time one of 'the mob', but often the magic power of three stripes made them forget those days. Generally speaking the sergeant 'on parade' was a far different fellow when off duty.

FOUND OUT
It was wonderful how the man in the ranks tumbled to the little weaknesses of his platoon sergeant and played on it accordingly, but on the other hand the NCO was not asleep and weighed up his flock. It amused me, and I often studied the various expressions, of how certain orders and commands worked on the troops. Just have a look at my nice little pictures on the previous page and you will understand. These are all from real life. Deepest depression! Joy! And sadness, also gladness and badness. All have a say. Leave! Your ticket and, of course, 'fatigue'. 'Private Wilson! You report at 6.30am. Latrine fatigue!' See his face! 'Me, Sergeant?' 'Yes! You.' No error.

HOLDING THE SCALES
Then he was supposed to know everything. All kinds of favours, requests and under the table suggestions were put to him. Could he do this, or that, or something else? Holding the scales always between the platoon officer and his men.

SERGEANT WM KELLY
There was one sergeant (Kelly by name) and I'll never forget him – the r*****!! He never missed me for any dirty work – and, yet, on the quiet we were old chums. A fine chap, Billy, and upright and true.

I often rowed against him (in fun of course) and said when I was made a sergeant major I would make 'him' hop, but I never got the chance.

So here's to the jolly old sergeant!

AND THE OTHERS

It was my good luck to meet and see quite a lot of other troops during the Great War. You can follow me in my short summary of a few impressions and sketches gained during my travels in France and Belgium.

### THE IRISH			All the world knows.
North, South, East or West, they were fine troops. Great 'storm troops'. Some regiments did not fancy too much red tape and were better in the war zone than on home service. All the world knows how the Irish boys can fight. They maintained that record during 1914-18 and I cannot single out any battalion for special mention. All were class.

SCOTTISH   What would we do?

What we would have done without them, the L*** only knows. Grim, determined lads. I know and understand their love of country. Attackers or in the defending role, Jerry always found them hard nuts to crack. Not given to half as much grousing as our English friends. Great troops.

ENGLISH

Some very fine fellows indeed in the English regiments. My choice would be the boys from the Midlands. To me the southern troops were 'softer' than the lads from 'oop North'. Climatic upbringing? Did not strike me as having, say, the dash of 'the Irish' but would accept hard discipline with better grace than us – and easier to handle. Groused a lot, yet carried on and were stubborn when cornered. Good Lads!

WELSH   Rugged fellows

Did not meet many, so cannot say much. What I did see of them left the impression that 'these would be rugged fellows in a scrap'.

THE FRENCH   Impulsive

Quick impulsive fellows. Excitable; good I would say when the day was going well for them, but for defence I should not place too much reliance on them. They had all kinds of troops in France from their dominions, dark, brown and black. Some good fighters here and tough customers in close work.

BELGIUM   Not robust

Different men from the French. Small as a rule, they did not look very robust, but held their end up fairly well. I don't think much love was lost between the French and them, so far as I could make out. They suffered cruel wrong in the Great War.

THE YANKS   Half Irish or Scotch

Some great lads here! Most of them came from English, Irish and Scottish stock, mostly Irish. Put in some real good work, but did not win the war. I think more of them could have been used, some in fact after months 'out there' never got firing a shot even, much to their disgust.

CANADA   Simply 'it' in a fight

Sturdy fellows! Not too well disciplined, but 'it' in a fight, good to know they were near at hand. Again their fathers and mothers were mostly from the old homeland.

NEW ZEALAND   Splendid men

The finest looking men in the British Army. Very gentlemanly and quiet. Fighters all, they never failed.

AUSTRALIANS   Dashing, happy-go-lucky

Dashing, happy-go-lucky chaps. They could not stick red tape of any kind. Some 'bad boys amongst them' but 99 per cent real gold. 'Say Buddy!' Not liked by the Huns, with good reason.

SOUTH AFRICA   Looked Good

Cannot pass any or, at least, very little criticism. Looked good, hard and staunch. Fought well on the Somme.

PORTUGUESE   Poor Stuff

Poor material and should never have been brought to the Western Front. Held in 'contempt' by the Germans. Washed out near Ypres.

THE GERMANS   Tough Fighters

Let me say right here that 'the enemy' were good soldiers. Generally overawed by their superior officers and browbeaten. Better fighters in the mass than in small lots. My order of merit would be 'the machine gunners first, then the bombers'. I don't think they were ever quite as good after the first Somme battle. Some of the spirit had gone – gone forever. Gradually got worse as the war came to an end, but if the Allies had not come to the help of France it would have been a picnic for the Germans and France would now be flying the black cross flag. No wonder she is still talking SECURITY.

A foe to be feared and worth watching.

DARK DAYS

1916 CAME IN WET AND MISERABLE

The little book has an entry to say this was a very hard time on the troops. Rain, snow and generally severe conditions. Moving from village to village, stopping a day here, a few somewhere else, sleeping tonight in a wood, tomorrow night in a bundle of hay, the next in a cold damp cellar, and then a spell in some old outhouse, to be followed with one or two beneath the stars. A roving life. Soaked to the skin on the march, we dried ourselves as best we could, often getting up to start the day in cold, damp, dirty and smelling clothes. Roughing it – at its best. Only the fittest men could survive it – but most of us were fit – fit and as hard as nails. Yet we never had a cold! Strange this, to look back on, because, since being demobbed in 1920, I know hundreds of the boys, and we suffer from this complaint. The sights and scenes still stand out in my memory as I again look back and see those little red-roofed villages we passed through. Happy days too!

BOOTS, BOOTS!

HOW THEY MOVE!

On the left flank, outside man of four, on the road – marching – marching along. In front of me as far as the eye can reach I see them, those BOOTS. How they swing in perfect unison, but as the day wears on I take an interest in the boots of the man in front. Why can't I look at something else? They simply draw me back. What will happen if he goes out of step? Will it trip me, will I fall down and not be able to rise again? Why have I such thoughts! Ah! He is starting to bob about. I'll be floored yet! Steady chum in front, keep up. Left! Left! Left! Good lad, just watch your step.

BIG RED SPOTS!

What's wrong with my eyes? Red spots on the pack of the man before me. Red – red spots. Getting bigger too! Hell, I pull myself together and looked down; his boots are red too. How heavy my kit is, the rifle sweats, the strap of the pack cut into the flesh; I pant for breath. Move to the left. Convoy coming – blast them. Splash, swish. To hell with those lorries. Ah! What a dowsing I get. Black water and mud, right in the face.

'I'M SAVED. HIS BOOTS ARE BLACK AGAIN.'

– BOOTS – BOOTS – BOOTS –

J. Maultsaid
1916

Star Shell Reflections 1914–1916

DREAMING ...

SAILING away up in the clouds. Yes! Right up amongst them, but not in an aeroplane. Oh dear, no! Lovely tea (that did not taste like soup), home-made bread, real butter and real jam. My! It's nice.

MALONE OR ORMEAU?

'Will we go for a walk dear?' 'Yes! Jim.' 'The Malone, or Ormeau?' 'It doesn't matter.' I take her arm and off we go.

HOT WATER BOTTLE

Beautiful clean sheets, a hot water bottle, and don't call me please until 10.00am. Then bring up the breakfast. All right!

WE WILL GET THEM

Shoot! Shoot! The Blues are pressing. Go on, Marshal. Ah! Bob why did you do that? I told you so – seven minutes and the Glens [Glentoran FC, another Belfast football club] are one up. No luck today, but we will get them again.

JUST DREAMING

I wonder what wee Minnie is doing now? Just her time for getting out from school, and the old mother? God bless her, come on, Corporal, it's time for relief. What the *****? I shake myself. My, it's cold! DREAMS …

RAIL BUILDERS

HEAVE – HO, all together there. It's a heavy lift, a big rail and some dozen of the boys underneath it.

'Say Corporal, what do they take us for?' 'I'm d***** if I know.' Rodgers sweated and cursed, and so did the rest of my squad, but orders are orders and we must get on with the good work. And the work? Making a railway. Snakes alive, what do we know about railways. Pull your weight there, Rooney! Tom glowered and pulled.

These were the days before the labour battalions gave the infantryman a chance to rest; we had to fight and work too in those days. Real manual hard labour this. Ballast, rails, sleepers. Pushing, hauling and hammering in iron pegs.

Down go the big sleepers, then the rails and the sledgehammer men go into action. Smash! Smash! 'What the H***?' 'Mind your D*** feet! Keep them clear.' A big stout RE gives orders (a private, too). The squad resent this. I intervene and calm the troops. We make slow progress, but creep onward. Sore in all parts, both body and soul we toil.

Rogers grumbles – give me the trenches any old time. I smile! Yes! Next week.

RAILWAYMEN

HEAVE-HO YOU

THE LITTLE ENGINE PUFFED UP AND DOWN.

ROGERS SWEATED AND CURSED.

MY TOES YOU D— FOOL

OH!

ROGERS GRUMBLES

GIVE ME THE TRENCH
I SMILE
YES!
NEXT WEEK.

Jim Maultsaid.

WHERE WE GOT THE "DOINGS" FROM.   SOMETIMES.

"DADDY" McBRIDE AND BIG BILLY BOWDEN STU[...] IN WITH HALF A STAIR[...]

Story FIREWOOD. NEXT PAGE.

"FIREWOOD"

FIREWOOD

ALL of us were starving. No.14 Platoon shivered in its boots. Cold inside and out. No firewood, no coke! What a war! What did we do to deserve all this? 'Daddy' McBride says he can get the stuff. All ears are eagerness. Good! Lead on father, but he was in no hurry. Oh! 'We must wait until it gets dark – dark in an hour or so and then leave it to me.' We left him to it, and his two cronies, Lewis 'the Kid', and big Bowden.

Sure enough, it turned up. I made a close examination of the wood. It was part, if not the whole, of a complete stairway! 'Where did you get it, old man?' 'Ask no questions Corporal, come along and warm yourself.' Gladly enough, I obeyed. It was a glorious blaze, far too glorious in fact, as Lieutenant Monard popped in to see if the old cellar was on fire. 'No sir, it's quite all right.'

Dixie lids were boiling, old overcoats drying and steam filled the room. Crash! Down the steps slid Lewis with half a sideboard or piece of some furniture on top of him. 'In the name of H*** where did you get that?' 'Oh! It was sitting outside – outside the billet.' 'I don't think so!!!'

THE RATION PARTY SINGLE FILE

RATION & WORKING PARTY. AT THE BEGINNING OF COMMUNICATION TRENCH ON THIR WAY TO WORK.

Just like the red men, we are all strung out. Each man has a sandbag over each shoulder, loaded like pack mules, rifle, ammunition and equipment thrown in.

After midnight and we clatter along. Funny to see the fairy-like icicles glistening in the frosty air. How sweet the air is. Sandbags are heavily loaded, biscuits, bully beef, coke, sticks, and other things, all for the boys in the line. The guns rumble away to the left – louder and louder – some poor devils getting it in the neck tonight. 'Keep quiet there!' Turn left, and here we are. The sky turned red away in front – brighter and brighter – then dies down.

It's a funny world too! Sleep is asking me to pay heed. I shake my body, and shake again. I itch! Blast those bugs! Could the frost not kill them? A wild desire to take off my shirt and give them a dose of frost takes hold on my brain. But impossible here. How the sky lights up – Boom! Boom! Boom! Yes! It's some war tonight, 'somewhere on the Western Front'.

The frost sparkles like silver, the stars shine. A strange world. Cold – cold – cold, but the L★★★ be praised, we can walk over the mud. What a glorious relief!

DING – DONG – DELL

THE SERGEANT'S IN THE WELL

Ding Dong Dell, the sergeant's in the well. Laugh – we laughed till we could not laugh any more.

'HELP! HELP!' A wild rush and we land outside. Pitch dark. Where is that awful cry coming from? Here it is! Where? We peer down! Yes, the black depths of the French well. Covered and boarded in. Just beside the wall of the little house, we were ignorant of its existence until this moment, and the voice? It's Sergeant - - - - - - - -.

'Help me for G★★★'s sake, boys.'

Knowing he was far from being dead, the boys simply roared with laughter. It took us several minutes to get a light struck and looked down. A white face peered up. He was ten or fifteen feet down – down in that evil-smelling damp mud, and sinking slowly.

Long boards were produced and pushed down. He grabbed them. What a job to get him hauled, but we managed. What a sight! A big man he was. Badly shaken, it was a case for the MO [Medical Officer] and we carried him there.

Result. Sergeant - - - - - - - - went down the line and No. 14 Platoon knew him no more.

DING-DONG-DELL.

LONG BOARDS WERE PUSHED DOWN

Nº 14 PLATOON KNEW HIM NO MORE

THE FRENCH CIRCUS

WE WERE AMUSED

To us it was a sight never to be forgotten, this French convoy. Just like the circus that you meet in this country of ours. We gave it the nickname on the spot 'The Circus'.

Carts of all shapes and sizes. Big, yes! Very big wheels. Vans. Loads of hay. Long vans of wooden pales. Horses and mules. A couple of goats trotting by the side of the big wagon was really comic. In fact it was no more like a military turnout than a parade before the fair in some country town in the Highlands of Donegal and would have given our Commanding Officer a blue fit on his tour of inspection. And the men! Long beards, unshaven and dirty. And the horses! A good feed would have killed some of them. We gazed in utter astonishment as this outfit rolled past. At first I thought the Germans had broken through their line at some point and this was their 'getaway'.

Nothing of the kind. It was a regular French army turnout. They waved and grinned at us, we laughed back. Certainly this was a strange sight in this country of surprises.

And the 'circus' passed by!

WE GREETED THEM AS THEY PASSED

A 'BLACK' IN THE BATH

He would have a bath – no matter what we said – but he didn't! Not that night anyhow.

THE BATH HOUSE
Back from the line we were, as usual, dirty and unkempt. In our back yard we moved around looking for somewhere to make a bathhouse and in doing so the landlady made it clear to us that the operation would not be tolerated by her. Objections did not hinder us; we 'carried on'. Two big tubs were made by cutting up water barrels, and the hot water made ready.

A BRAVE MAN
None of us was keen to start as there was danger in the air. Eagle eyes watched us from cover. Stanley Black declared that he would chance it and d*** the old lady. Brave lad! Crash! Smash! Ear-splitting sounds from below No. 14 Platoon tumbled down the stairs. Madame held a hurricane lamp above her head and her good husband wielded a large axe. What a sight! And what a rage they were in! Cat like, we made the advance, when out flashed a figure in nature's garb, sprinted across the yard to disappear like a flash up the stairs.

ON GUARD
An armed sentry took up duty. The boys had their bath, but not Stanley. Oh! Dear no – he is trembling yet!

THE STOKES FAMILY

This brotherhood was very unpopular with the line battalions and the cause was this.

DUTY FINISHED THEY DISAPPEARED

A certain point in the enemy front line was picked out (from the map I suppose) as we did not see or know anything about them until one fine afternoon a bunch of men came along with strange guns and strange pouches containing large shells. Some adjustments were made, then, Swish! Clash! Bang! Fast as they could send it across, these shells were hurled at our 'friends' across the way. Forty or fifty crashed and smashed into poor Jerry's front line. Hot stuff this! Yes! Very hot – but wait! Their duty done, it took them but several minutes to pack up and clear out. Yes! Good work, no doubt.

A PRESENT FROM KRUPPS

But wait. We hadn't looked a minute or more on their backs when, to our horror and disgust, Jerry replied in his best manner to our greetings. Half of Krupps' foundry was thrown at us, and the Stokes family were not there to meet it. Ever after we loved them.

THE REs

AS they say in the kiddies' books of learning – RE stands for Royal Engineer. Fine fellows, no mistake about that, but, and there is always a 'but', they were nearly as popular as the sergeant major, and everyone knows how he was liked.

REPORT AT DUCKHOUSE FARM
I think we were taken for 'navvies' by these gentlemen, not fighting men.

You will report to Sergeant - - - - - of the REs at 6.00am at 'Duck House Farm' with twenty-five men. Iron rations to be carried (iron, mind, a good name; the man who called them this knew a thing or two). Well! Anyhow, we find ourselves at the mercy of that RE gent for a whole day. What gloom! He hands out the 'dope' and some shovels and picks too, and retires (where I don't know). 'What did you say Corporal?'

I said we have to make a dug-out right here. So many feet deep etc., etc.

This order did not help to make me any more popular, but no help for it my lads. Just get 'stuck into it'.

McCLAY AND ROONEY GROUSE
This b***** show must be for a general, grumbles McClay, and Rooney agrees. May the L*** bless the REs and keep them from harm, says big Bowden, as he drags an iron girder after him.

'KID' LEWIS TO INVENT A DIGGER
After much sweating the troops have dug deep in the good red soil of France and 'Kid' Lewis swears if he lives he will invent a 'steam digger' for the next war 'to save the poor soldiers' this heart-breaking business.

FOR SIR DOUGLAS HAIG
The RE overseer turns up. Not deep enough. Three more feet. 'Say chum,' I ask, 'Is this for Sir Douglas Haig and his staff? I never met anything like this on my travels 'up there' did you?' This was sarcastic on my part. 'None of your cheek my lad or I'll send in a report.' 'Yes! I suppose you are pretty good at that, better than ... .' I kept the rest to myself. We toil, and boil, but made a good job of that blasted dug-out.

DRYING IN

Army slang for the art of being able to disappear in the critical moment – that moment being when an NCO appeared in the offing to pick up a fatigue party.

IT WAS AN ART – in fact it was a trade

We had our share of these experts in No.14 Platoon. In fact some of them were so expert they could 'smell' a fatigue squad a hundred yards away and, like the old soldier in the song, just fade away. 'Dodging the column' was another slang phrase meaning much the same thing. Of course it was more difficult to 'miss' the work when his name was on the list, but sick parade was a 'get out'. Even a dose of the famous number nine pill [a laxative] was easier to some than a bit of hard graft.

Now these gentry were not unknown to the NCOs who often got accounts squared in a quiet way, to our secret joy. This was only fair to the honest boys who did not shirk, and were not using a few stripes as a cloak for mean or petty revenge.

A cute lot – these 'column dodgers'.

GRUESOME

NOT SO BAD IN THE DAYTIME BUT WHEN THE SHADOWS FELL!

SKETCH FROM ACTUAL SPOT BY. JIM MAULTSAID 1916.

GRUESOME

DOWN AMONG THE BONES
To say the least of it, our next spell in line was a strange experience and we lived (my squad and I) down – down in amongst those who had long, long ago passed out – among the bones of French citizens laid to rest many years before in a little quiet country village.

HORRIBLE
Horrible no doubt, but our front line and reserve trenches ran through the old graveyard and all we could do was make the best of it.

NOT HAPPY
Many I knew in my lot did not feel happy, no more did I, and often in the night watches I pictured those souls coming back to haunt this place, to make a protest against us, 'the intruders', for disturbing their sleep. Often in our bit of dug-out we disturbed the bones, and the shells churned up more when the guns played on us. Huh! I did not like it at all, at all. War is hell! We felt like living in 'it' during the seven days.

A SHOCK.
FOR CORPORAL JIM

=== PICTURES BELOW ===

TO SAY THAT I WAS ASTONISHED PUTS IT MILDLY — THEY SAT THERE — THOSE TWO — ALL ALONE WHAT WERE THEY DOING HERE?

A SHOCK FOR CORPORAL JIM

Night was falling. We were on way to the firing line and getting quite close. Something compelled me to scramble up the side of the trench and look over. Why, I don't know.

ASTONISHED

To say I was astonished puts it mildly. They sat there, those two, all alone. What were they doing here? I knew they were relieving the Skins, but this pair had no earthly right to be in this little house, it was a very small one, and playing cards too! What nerve. Yet how quiet and composed they looked.

WHAT A DROP!

It was too much for me. I must investigate this business. Telling my section to move on slowly, but leaving one or two to await my return, I scrambled out, up and over. Advancing at the 'on guard', rifle loaded, I crept up to the door and peered in. Not a move did these men make. Not from our division, the shoulder colours told me that. Lord, but they were quiet! Never a move. Never a sound. Hands up! I cried. Not a movement! Straight in, I went. Two dummy figures dressed in our uniform.

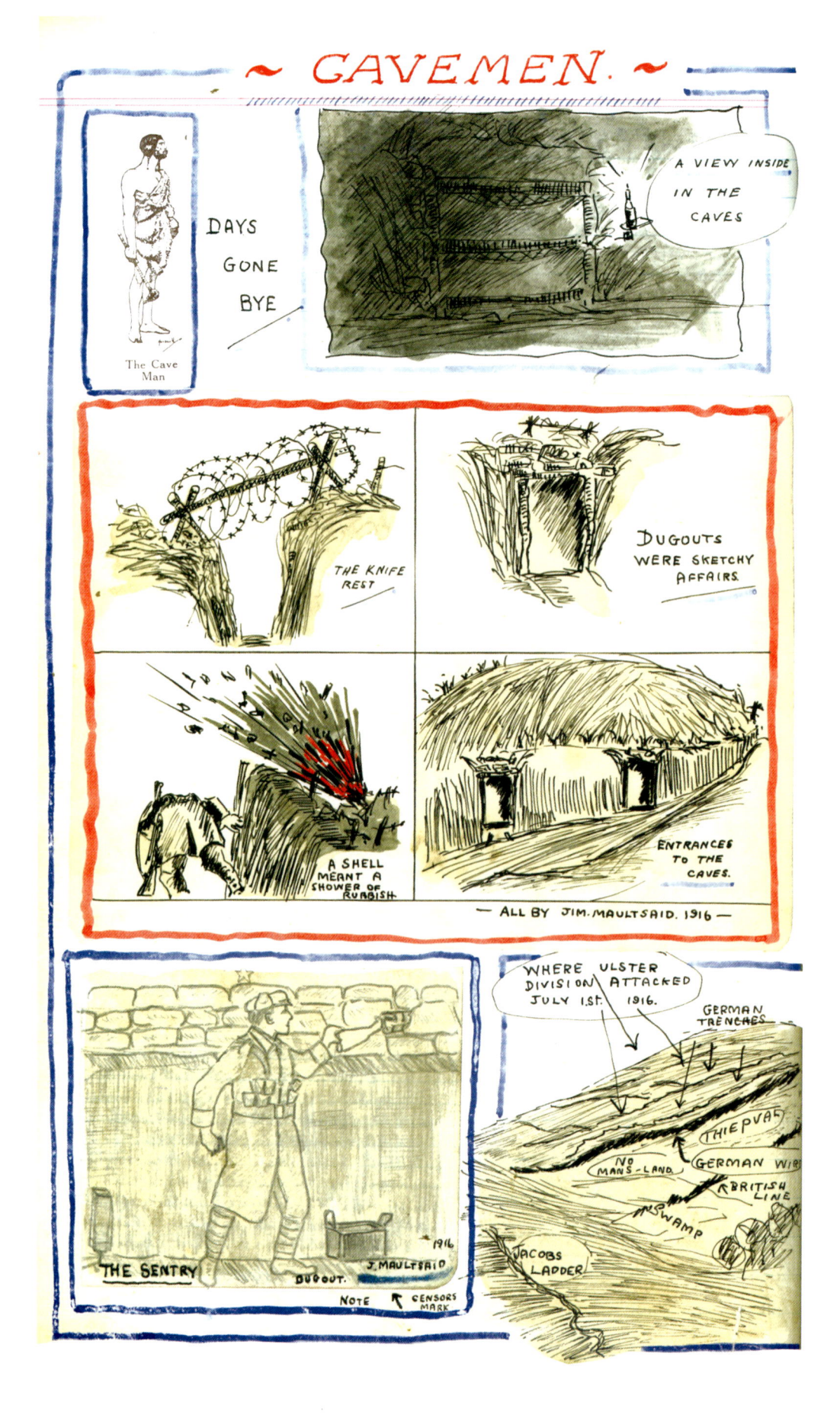

~ CAVEMEN. ~

The Cave Man

DAYS GONE BYE

A VIEW INSIDE IN THE CAVES

THE KNIFE REST

DUGOUTS WERE SKETCHY AFFAIRS.

A SHELL MEANT A SHOWER OF RUBBISH.

ENTRANCES TO THE CAVES.

— ALL BY JIM. MAULTSAID. 1916 —

THE SENTRY   DUGOUT.   J. MAULTSAID 1916
NOTE ↑ CENSORS MARK

WHERE ULSTER DIVISION ATTACKED JULY 1st. 1916.
GERMAN TRENCHES
THIEPVAL
NO MANS-LAND
GERMAN WIRE
BRITISH LINE
SWAMP
JACOBS LADDER

CAVEMEN

CHALK EARTH WAS EVERYWHERE
A couple of feet down and you were into the chalk. White as snow. Sandbags were filled with it, and the trenches dug in it. Looking out on the German lines your eye could trace them for miles, thin long strands of gleaming whiteness set in a black background. You could trace it all as it stood out in bold relief, their network of reserve and communication systems. Many a time I studied them from Jacob's Ladder – a section of our trenches named after the Bible – and looked out on those enemy strongholds away on our right in front of Thiepval, name of sorrow, never dreaming that one day I would cross that little black strip of land between the woods and Jerry's line, and cross it with chums who would never come back. But! This is another story at another time.

NOT A PLEASANT SPOT
Not a pleasant part of the line this. Clay was scarce. Old rubbish of all sorts was used as barricade stuff, and the knife-rest type of defence was much in evidence. A shell meant a shower of bricks, chalk and rubble. Dangerous stuff flying about.

SKETCHY SHELTERS
Dug-outs were hard to make and the ones made were skeleton ones. You had the sensation here of being helpless against any gunfire. Strange to say, I looked at this spot from the German lines on 1 July and marvelled at the position we once held.

LIVING LIKE RABBITS
Just about where our 'reserves' took up quarters there was a chalk hill or large mound. This was a perfect network of underground caves. We had burrowed in and in like rabbits, or was it the French? Quite easy to get lost here. Beds were cut out from the chalk, bomb stores, ration stores, ammunition dumps all had a place in this big house under the hill. Safe enough here.

How strange it all was. Living like our forefathers thousands of years ago, and the rats. Huh! There in their thousands, and the smell of it all! To me it lives forever.

JUST CAVEMEN
Cavemen we were, just as in ages long, long ago. History repeats itself?

NEW TERRORS

ABOUT this time we were introduced to some of Jerry's heaviest and most ugly form of trench bombardments in the shape of big 'Jack Johnsons' [German 150mm shells; they were named after Jack Johnson, the first African-American world heavyweight champion as they were black in colour], *minenwerfers'* [literally mine launchers, German heavy mortars] whizz-bangs, rifle grenades etc., etc.

How we 'used to watch' (this is an Ulster dialect) the big black tin cans sail up in the air, curve down and crash on our trenches. All the world was mad! Our eardrums almost split asunder as we held our breath and waited … waited for what? Eternity perhaps! God! It was awful to stand, to crouch, to fall flat, to grasp your rifle in a fearful grip, and wait: dodge, shake and gasp for air; was your heart still in the same place? It pounded, hammered in your brain – thump – thump – thump. Nerves were on edge, raw, jumpy and all out of gear. Thank God, I had ones of iron and kept control of myself.

NEW TERRORS

WATCHING "IT" COMING.
THEN DOWN —

THERE SHE COMES!

There she comes! Yes, straight down on us. We are thrown yards away, crashed up against the back of the trench all in a heap. My nose bleeds. I feel myself all over. Still safe, no bones broken. What a flash, what a roaring sound, as if the very heavens had fallen apart. Picking myself up, I am surprised to see the bottom of the trench littered with razorblades, horseshoe nails, scrap iron, and bits of glass. What a war!

This form of projectile was thrown at us by some kind of trench mortar. The only (good?) point was that we got half a chance to dodge it, as it was visible in the air. Of course when coming over like hailstones this was impossible.

AT OVER 100 MPH

'Big coal-boxes' [a heavy German shell, the name came from the black smoke when it burst] or 'Jack Johnsons' came over with a swish like an express train passing at 100 mph and kicked up a big black cloud of dark black suffocating smoke. My word, they made us choke.

LIGHT AND DEADLY

Whizz-bang [a German high velocity shell]. Well and truly was this shell named. It was on top of you in a flash. Light, quick and deadly in the open, but not great in the destruction of trench or earthworks for all that nasty missile. They came in lots of four, just Flash! Flash! Flash! Flash! No time to dodge death.

HAPPY HOURS

COME BACK ~ AGAIN ~

HAPPY HOURS

Joy and Sadness
How we loved the mail to arrive. It was a sight to see the boys scramble round the company postman. What joy! What sadness! 'Nothing for me today?' 'No!' How the old heart sank. 'Any for me?' 'Yes! Here's two.'

A quiet corner in the straw, the old candle splutters and you tear open your letter from home. My, it was sweet, and the parcels: I can still bring the thrill back it gave me to cut the string and see what the package contained. A neat little cake (cake, and no mistake). Sweets and other little luxuries. Gee! It's good to be alive.

WHAT'S WRONG CHUM?

He is silent in the corner. What's wrong chum? Bad news? Yes, a loved one somewhere on the home front has gone forever. We express our sympathy, but the pain remains for weeks and months. Such is life.

A DEEP PLOT

'Listen to me, Corporal. Do you notice that - - - - - never gets a letter or parcel!' 'No, I did not.' 'What about making one up?' 'That's a fine idea.' We plot and plan and have a whip round. The package is given to the orderly postman and duly delivered.

What surprise and joy!

THE CRUCIFIX

AS WE TURN THE CORNER

THE CRUCIFIX

They stood at every corner and often by the wayside. Large, small, magnificent, poor, all classes, some of wood, but mostly wrought iron. Like sentinels of the dead they stood in the graveyards, and they guarded every place of worship. How often did our battalion orders read 'Meet at Crucifix corner'? How many times was this word mentioned? Millions I should say, and the battles often raged around them, the signboards read again and again the familiar word. Every little hamlet had its own – and all stood out in some prominent position. How symbolic of France – in this, 'the hour of her own crucifixion!'

THE CROSS

There was a something pathetic to see the form of our Lord Jesus Christ on the cross and us, marching, yes, marching to WAR and, yet again, was it a sign implying and saying to us 'all ye that labour, come unto me, and I will give you rest'?

MENTAL PHOTOGRAPH

In the closing down of the day, as the evening shadows fall, we turn the corner of that little village – and there before us stands the Crucifix. The impression is photographed on our brains, to last forever.

THE LUCKY ONE

NOT ME. Oh! Dear. No! But we often 'dreamed' about it, talked about it and joked, but the good fortune was never mine to get 'leave' from the Battalion. Still, some of the boys somehow managed it; how I don't know, but manage it they did. The troops had a joke to the effect that you had to be in the transport, at the base, or at headquarters before you had a 'dog's chance' to click.

It looked like it, I must confess, at times. I cannot bring to mind a No.14 Platoon man having the honour. Of course we were D Company and last on the list, then forgotten about. Was that it, I wonder? Or were the D Company men too useful?

David and Goliath.

No 14 Platoon Out of Luck.

WHAT I OFTEN PICTURED........
How I would look when that LEAVE (that never turned up) would come.

BY Corpl. Jim. Maultsaid
Somewhere in France
19-1-1916

WE WAVED GOOD BYE TO A MORE FORTUNATE CHUM.

BATTALION ORDERS

NO LEAVE FOR KELLY OR JOHNSTON!

ALL READY FOR THE LEAVE DRAFT

PICTURES ~ BY ~ JIM. MAULTSAID

THAT "BACK TO IT ALL AGAIN" FEELING

RELIEF'S
PICTURES ALL BY JIM. MAULTSAID.

BE CAREFUL A DANGEROUS CORNER

A TIGHT CRUSH —

WE "BATE" THE 9th SKINS 4-0 —

HERE THEY COME

HAVE YOU A CANDLE TO SPARE?

WE PASS OUT. DUTY OVER.

RELIEFS

An air of suppressed excitement ripples through the ranks. In a few minutes our relief battalion should be here. All our little odds and ends have been put together and stuffed into haversacks or tied to the equipment.

Will we get clear without a final strafe? [*Strafe* is a German word meaning 'punish' but was to become a military term for an attack, especially by aircraft.] One thing the boys did not like – and that was bombardment in the middle of 'relief'.

The trenches were packed with the incoming troops and the 'outward bound' lot had the devil of a time crushing past. In fact all the trench approaches were choked up, making it very unpleasant indeed.

A dull clattering of trench tools against the side of the trench warns us that our friends are now arriving (some hours late as usual). I stand back in a recess and meet the sergeant. 'Yes! This is D Company. Here you are, old man. Your front is from this bay to - - - - . It takes twenty-five men, and the "sap head" is along here. Be careful, a dangerous corner this.' 'Is Jerry quiet?' 'Well! fair. We had a bad night last night, but quiet since.'

RELIEFS

'Have you a candle to spare, Corporal?' 'Aye! Here's a bit of one; all I've got, but you can have it.'

DERRY AND BELFAST

The Derry tongue mixes well with the Belfast variety as we pass along, posting and changing the sentries. 'Man we had a 'quare' win last week. We 'bate' the 9th Skins 4-0.' 'Good! But wait until the YCVs get you! Six won't save you.' 'Ah! Get away wid you – don't you mind the day …'. But his reply was never given; we heard it coming and threw ourselves down – down in the mud.

The trench heaves and shakes. Lawk's alive but that was a near one. We pull ourselves up wipe the muck from our faces and 'carry on'.

KEEP LOW

'Here's the bomb store, there's six full boxes, that should keep you going. A weak spot in our wire just like there, and keep low as the snipers give this place hell all day long.'

10th SKINS TAKE OVER

'Well, chum, that's about all. See and take care of yourself.' I grasped the hand of the sergeant in the 10th Battalion Royal Inniskillings (Derry boys) and GO!

A SHOWER BATH NEW STYLE

FRIDAY was payday and it was a Friday night. Just out from the line, the troops had got rid of some or most of their hard-earned five francs in the wine shop – and needless to say most of them were 'happy'.

THE RED WINE OF FRANCE
The stairs were 'rickety' and 14 Platoon took 'some' putting up those stairs. The thin wine of France as a rule made them 'trot' during their sleeping hours, so some cute soldier had a brainwave and secured a big tin which was hauled up to the loft, to act as a urinal-bucket during the night. A very good idea indeed, if that tin had been a sound one – but – wait –

FLOODED OUT
Sergeant Major Du'Quest and myself found a little spot beneath the loft, just room enough for two, and down we snuggled, nice and comfortable. In the land of dreams I was when –

WOKE UP WITH A STARTLED CRY 'WE'RE DROWNING' – AND SURE ENOUGH IT WAS COMING DOWN IN TORRENTS – FROM THE ROOF –
Blankets soaked, wet through to the skin we scrambled up.

RAIN – YES, RAIN?
It was painful when we discovered where the 'rain' had come from – from that blasted loft up above. The big tin (or bin) had been used as a urinal convenience, filled up gradually until full up, then, *having no bottom*, the old rotten roof of the loft gave way, down came the 'deluge' on top of poor Du'Quest and 'yours truly'.

14 PLATOON 'STRAFED'
Never have I heard such language as my friend the company sergeant major spat out as I followed him up those rickety stairs to play the devil with No.14 Platoon.

'SERGEANT JIM'

Glad news for me when I read Corporal J. A. B. Maultsaid D Company

PROMOTED SERGEANT as from - - - - -
Of course the event had to be duly celebrated and I stood the bill – that was that – but when duly introduced to the 'upper ten' in the Sergeants' Mess 'put them up' once more in good spirit – not the spirit of the glass for, as I did not touch, taste, or handle alcohol in any shape or form (even the rum ration was refused by me) you can understand how cool and collected I managed to keep through all the celebrations.

PLEASED AND PROUD
Was I pleased? You can bet your life I was. I have worked hard, fought hard, learned hard and always obeyed my orders. Truth to tell, I meant to get on in this new life and may now tell you the secret. From the day I joined until the day I was demobbed, that was exactly five years and three months, I did not figure on the charge sheet even once, and I did not have occasion to bring any man before my superior officer even once. Now, I was not slack, far from that, in my duty but I studied my men, was very tactful, and never 'done' (army slang) the heavy stuff, just a little reason, a little chat, and, lo!, difficulties were simply smoothed away.

'The boys' on your side, you could have met or faced all the German army with confidence in your heart, knowing they would not let you down – AND THEY NEVER DID.

POOR JOE JOHNSTON
Joe Johnston (poor soul, he has since gone to join his mates of the old platoon up above) had to have the honour of sewing on my three stripes and make me, as he said, a real 'posh' sergeant.

THE GAS BAGS
SOMETIMES WE COUNTED HALF A DOZEN WATCHING - WATCHING US.
ANOTHER TYPE OF THE PEST.
WE OFTEN BLAMED THEM FOR A SHOWER OF SHELLS.
A VIEW THROUGH A POWERFUL TELESCOPE
A BRIGHT RED FLASH ! ... AND A PEST LESS TO WORRY US.
- JIM. MAULTSAID. -
A FAMILIAR BRAND

THE GAS BAGS

WE NEVER LIKED THE SIGHT OF THEM – THOSE BIG GAS BAGS
Swinging in the breeze away behind the German lines, watching, watching us all the time, from dawn till dusk, the 'invisible eye' on all our movements. Sometimes we could count as many as half a dozen, all in a line, all on the lookout.

'Spotters' for gun positions, troop movements, and anything out of the ordinary, no doubt they served the enemy well. We often blamed them for a shower of shells at unexpected points, and we were not far wrong.

UP GOES THE PEST
Our air force had some great fun in trying to dispose of these 'pests'. It was thrilling to see them sweep down, then a bright red flame would shoot up to the sky, and one less on the list to worry us; but only for a time as that space would be filled up next morning. Of course we had ours too, just to keep an eye on Jerry.

SPORTS DAY

ONE of the best sporting battalions in the army, that was the 14th Royal Irish Rifles (YCV), we had athletes of all kinds, scores of them. Runners, boxers, footballers (of both codes), jumpers, in fact any sport you could mention and we could find the talent to meet, and often defeat, any opposition from other battalions.

THE SECRET

From our earliest days way up in Finner we took every opportunity after the day's work was over to turn out for a match, a run, or a few rounds with the gloves. Our officers backed us up in every way and often took part in the games themselves, a fine example of sportsmanship. It was the same at Randalstown, at Seaford, at Bramshott, and in France and Belgium, in fact all the way through our history at home and abroad. This, in my opinion, was one of the secrets of our being able to 'stick it', all the hardships and the miseries of trench, dug-out and awful billets. We were 'fit', very, very fit indeed and fitness is half the battle in this life. Of course, the usual physical jerks played their part, but it is not this part of the programme I wish to speak about. No! They stood apart.

SUCCESS

Now, personally, I was an out and out 'sports merchant'. Boxing, running and the old love, football, claimed me on every possible occasion. I do not intend to bore you with my success (and sometimes non-success) on this page; you can read my record on another page and judge for yourself.

TRAINED ON MILK

I remember a budding heavyweight whom the cooks discovered and he was coaxed to train for a fight. They actually rubbed him down with condensed milk. Just think of it. A joke, no doubt, but if memory serves me correctly he went out and won. All power to the milk? What an advert for the makers!

SPORTS DAY IN FRANCE

This was a day in France, we had finished our turn in the line and 'sports' were to be held.

A large field was found (rented? I'm afraid not) but Sergeant Murphy and his fatigue squad got busy anyhow to prepare the field for track events, etc. Platoon sergeants took a list of names for each event and a programme was then drawn up. All ready for 'the day'.

SPORTS DAY

COME ON D COMPANY

The troops turned out. Company rivalry was red hot; it was always so. Come on A Company! Let's hear from you, B. What about C Company. Now then, D Company. Last as usual, but not when the prizes were being given out. My bunch were hot in the sports department, even if we were not much good at anything else. Yes, Sir! That was D Company.

SPORTS DAY.
~ SKETCES. ~
BY-JIM MAULTSAID-.
RUNNERS
BOXERS
FOOTBALLERS
JUMPERS
~ ALL SORTS OF TALENT ~
"A CLOSE-UP OF OUR CONDENSED MILK CHAMPIO
YOUR MILK SON
WHAT AN ADVT?
MILK
THE TROOPS TURNED OUT
— TO A MAN —
~ COME ON "D" COY ~
SEG'T COLE
—AND—
~HIS~
MULE.
"D" COY
TO THE FORE WHEN PRIZES WERE GIVEN OUT.
JIM. MAULTSAID. RE-DRAWN FROM MY SKET BOOK.

A FINE COMBINATION

How they yelled as I flashed home in the final of the NCOs' 220 yards sprint, or carried the baton past the post in the relay championship, bringing honour and renown to D Company. The personal pleasure was little to me, it was for my beloved company. Even yet I can bring to mind the famous combination of sprinters that upheld 'poor old D Company – Sergeant Kelly, Sergeant Powell, Sergeant Maultsaid and Bugler Mulholland, (poor boy, since gone home to rest). Yes! We could all 'move some' in those days.

SERGEANT COLE – CAN YOU FORGET?

Sergeant Cole on his mule (as Charlie Chaplin) lives in our mind for all time. How wise that mule was.

RINGING IN MY EARS YET

The obstacle race was a scream. Ah! Regimental Sergeant Major Elphic 'bossed the show'. Come on D Company! Come on! I can hear it yet.

OLD FAVOURITES

Here are a few we sang:

'Ulstermen MARCH! MARCH! MARCH! All together'

'Bridget Lie Close To The Wall'

'Nellie Dean by the Old Mill Stream'

'The Mountains Of Mourne'

'The South Down Militia, The Terrors of the Land'

'It's A Long Way To Tipperary'

'Old Soldiers Never Die'

'Pack All Your Troubles in Your Old Kit Bag'

'Only One More Kit Inspection For M'

'Just a Piece of 4 By 2'

'There's A Long Long Trail A-Winding'

'Only One More Church Parade Finis'

'I Don't Want to go to The Trenches'

SONG VISIONS

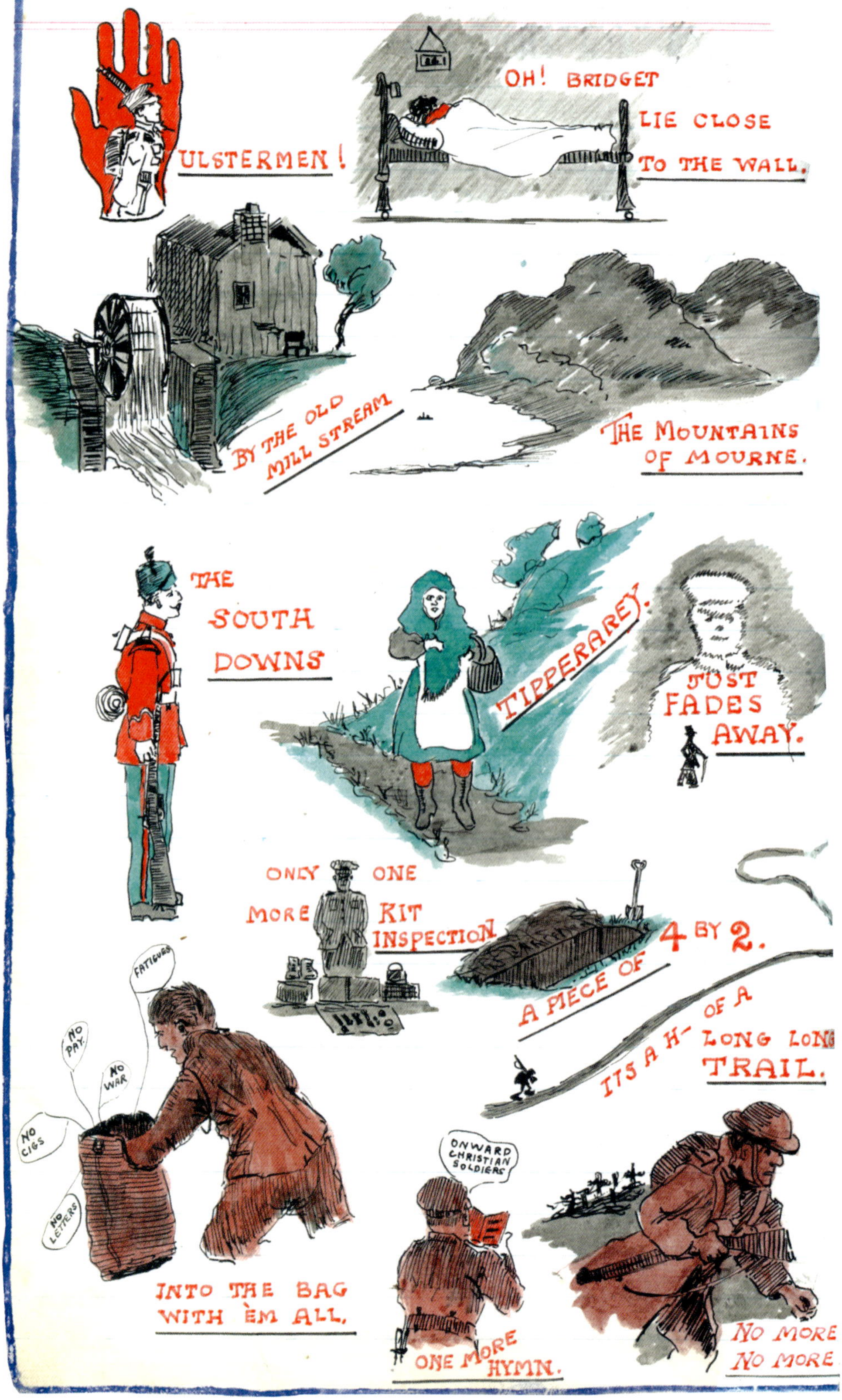

Every war had its own songs, and the Great War was no exception. In fact, during those hectic years 1914 to 1918 songs came in quick succession. Our battalion were strong singers and musical talent was plentiful. The leader in this branch was usually Sergeant Robert Stewart, he himself having a splendid voice. Songs that were 'sad' songs that were 'glad', and sometimes 'bad' all had their turn. To meet us in full marching order, in good form, was a treat, if we were giving one of our favourite songs. To hear those 'thousand voices' all together full out, and in part – well it was something to remember – and as I already said 'we had class singers' who could, and did, deliver the goods in this line. How a certain song can still bring back certain memories!

Can't you hear the boys even yet – at Southampton? Can't you still hear them as they tramp through the mud of France and Flanders? To the day I 'pass out' I'll still remember! Yes! Our boys could sing – I could not – but I enjoyed it thoroughly for all that.

WHERE IS THE 14TH MAN WHO WILL EVER FORGET?
'Bridget Lie Close to the Wall'

STRETCHER BEARERS

I CAN HEAR THAT CRY YET
When this word flashed from bay to bay (trench sections) we knew that there was some poor soul who needed removing to the first aid dressing station.

FULLY APPRECIATED
As the Great War progressed our respect and appreciation of the 'stretcher bearers' grew. These men worked under terrible difficulties at times, often risking their lives to rescue a chum from no man's land, or some awful section of the trench line that was being blown to atoms by the Huns. Then again the communication trenches were far too narrow, or full of turns that made the carrying of a loaded stretcher a nightmare. These Red Cross boys toiled and sweated under their mighty burden to save a life and bring some hope to a stricken, blood-stained, khaki-clad soldier, who once was a fine figure of a man but now was stricken down and in awful agony. Yes! These men were worthy of all the honour and praise that has been bestowed on them.

SEE THEM STRUGGLE
See them rushing round the trench on an urgent call!
   See them struggle through the mud, each step a torture!
   Again see those two figures, sweat blinding them, as they gently carry in their charge to lay him down at the first aid station and start all over again away up those miles of trenches! Thank goodness I did not belong to this section.

THROUGH THE MUD

JIM MAULTSAID 1916.

LANGTRY MCDOWELL

One of these boys that I often admired was Langtry McDowell of the 14th Royal Irish Rifles. Big, strong and always willing, he deserved all the medals that were ever issued for bravery, but if he was ever rewarded I cannot say. Often he toiled all through the night hours binding up ghastly wounds, taking a turn at 'carrying', working until he dropped down from sheer exhaustion. Just a sample of what the 'stretcher bearers' were.

GINGER McMULLEN

Red hair and a red – I nearly said character – but no! He was a rough diamond, no error, but for all his faults he was 'fearless'.

WHERE DID D COMPANY GET THEM?

The famous D Company possessed some 'rare' and 'strange' characters. 'Wild' and a little 'Woolly', all had their special characteristic points – good and bad.

    Among the wild variety I'll place our friend Ginger McMullen. He stood out on his own. Not a man in the whole Battalion that did not know and hear of his exploits.

GINGER McMULLEN

"OUT ON HIS OWN"

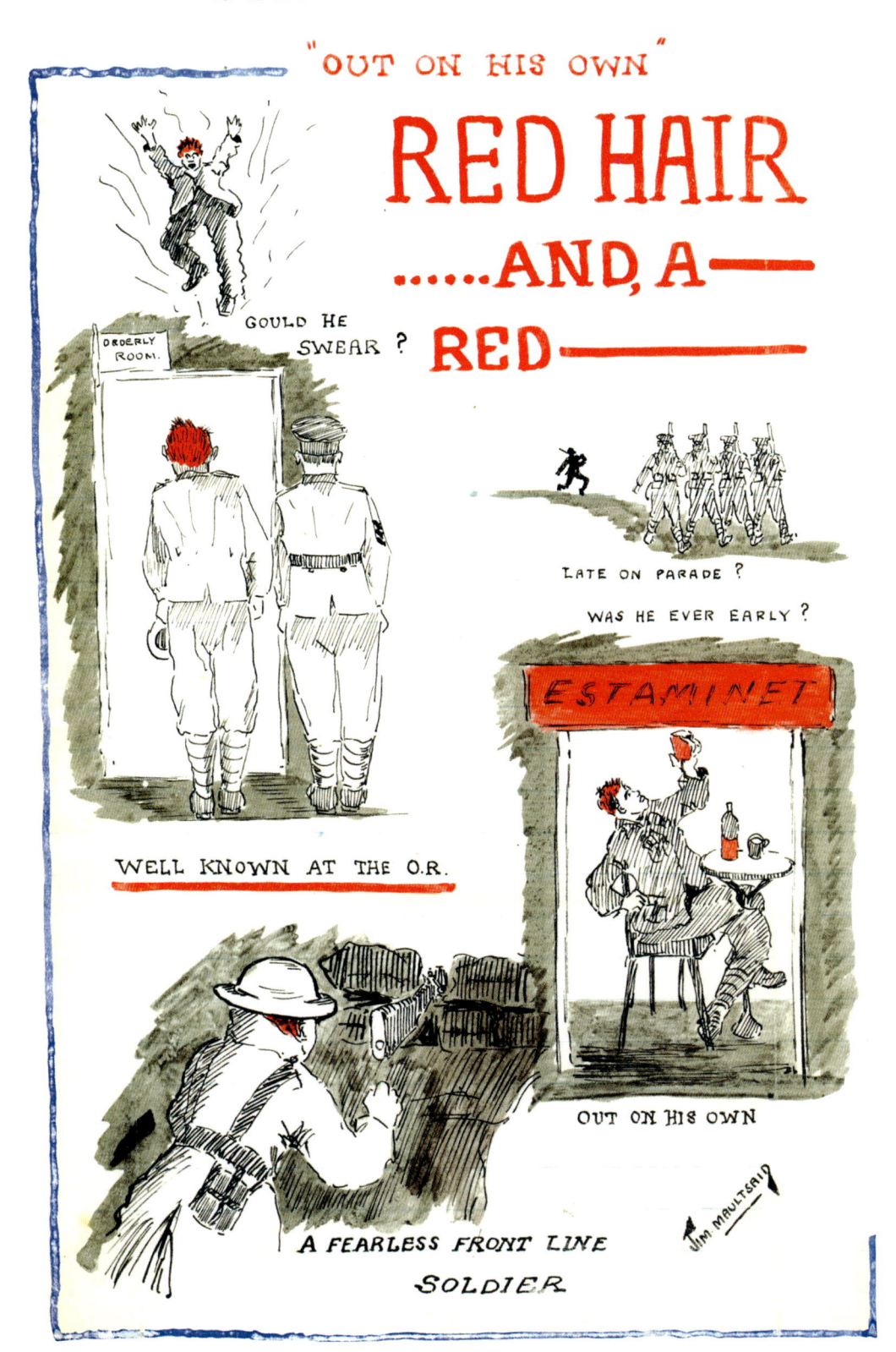

RED HAIR
......AND, A
RED————

COULD HE SWEAR?

LATE ON PARADE?

WAS HE EVER EARLY?

WELL KNOWN AT THE O.R.

ESTAMINET

OUT ON HIS OWN

A FEARLESS FRONT LINE SOLDIER

Jim Maultsaid

COULD HE?

Could he swear? Ye gods! Preserve me!

Could he take a drink???????????????

And late on parade? Was he ever early?

And grouse! Perpetual motion solved.

Did he hold his own up? Never failed.

Poor Captain Willis once told him 'he was a hardened criminal' (this was not in civilian sense – but his army record).

With all his 'little' faults, Ginger was a fearless front-line soldier.

HIS BIBLE

HE LOVED HIS GOD

One of the most God-fearing men I ever met was Joseph Montgomery.

If ever a man was sure of a place up above it was Joe. Honest, upright and true, he was a real Christian in every way. By word and action he set us an example and his little sermons always carried weight.

I CAN SEE HIM YET

The candle splutters. Several of the boys are playing cards, some reading, others writing home. Joe is reading his little Bible. I can see him yet in tent, billets, and dug-out as he passed the final paragraph, finish, close 'the book', place it under his pillow, then get down on his knees and say his prayers to his heavenly Father.

'JOE' BY J.M. 1915

J.M. 1916.

I CAN SEE HIM YET

HIS REWARD

I never heard him swear or take the Lord's name in vain. I never knew him to do an unkind action or grasp any unfair opportunity. Older than us, we looked up to him, and in our hearts we all admired his fine courage – always looking upwards. Poor Joe's body lies in Flanders but his soul is with his heavenly Father.

THE SKINS

WHY THE 14TH ROYAL IRISH RIFLES WERE PUT INTO A FUSILIER BRIGADE I CANNOT SAY, BUT A FINER LOT OF FELLOWS THAN OUR FRIENDS THE SKINS YOU COULD NEVER MEET DERRY – DONEGAL – TYRONE – AND FERMANAGH – ALL TOGETHER

It was a surprise to find ourselves in a Fusilier Brigade, us, our Rifle Regiment, but let me say right here that our chums the 9th, 10th and 11th Royal Inniskilling Fusiliers were the finest lot of 'bhoys' one could have ever wished to meet. 'Phawt are you talking about?' 'Shure, an' ye are talking blarney!' Now I'm just 'spaking' the native tongue.

Yes! It was broad, very broad indeed. On every side you heard it, the rich deep voice from 'ould Donegal', broadsides from Tyrone or Fermanagh and the Derry tongue – once heard, never forgotten. What a mixture, and here we were (the Belfast men) right amongst it all. At first we were not understood and got the nickname at Finner 'The Chocolate Soldiers'.

This arose from the fact, I think, that most of our lot lined up at the canteen for buns, lemonade and chocolate and the Skins lined up for a beer. Not that some of our lads could or would not lower a pint with the best of them, but as a rule we were TT.

SPORT DRAWS US CLOSER

In the world of sport a new and better understanding arose. They grew to respect our prowess and this brought us very much closer – closer indeed as the years rolled past – until we fought side-by-side in France and Belgium. Then indeed we were friends for ever; there was no one, or no lot, like the YCVs. And us? We loved them all, those big fearless fellows, fellows that feared no foe. A wonderful friend, and a deadly enemy.

NOT KNOWN TO THEM

The humble opinion of yours truly is that no better or braver men ever landed on the shores of France. They can fight, and did fight with magnificent courage – never retreated – and never knew the meaning of the word 'retire'.

QUICK RETURN

I can bring to mind that dark night in 1916 when they were rushed up to Thiepval Wood to send Jerry's raiding party back all in a hurry – less some scores of men killed and prisoners that they held on to – and this was to assist the South Wales Borderers.

"TYPICAL INNISKILLINGS"

"The Skins cleared Jerry out of that wood in no time"

FROM "OULD DONEGAL"

A TYPICAL DERRYMAN

"All night long the Skins lay out in No-Mans-Land in the sunken road"

"They never failed to bring in several prisoners from a raid."

SKETCHES BY JIM MAULTSAID FROM SKETCH BOOK

AN OFFICER FROM TYRONE

FERMANAGH

BRINGING IN THE GREY BOYS

Then their raiding parties were a sore thorn in the Hun's side. Sharp and deadly, they worked havoc amongst the German trenches, to return with a 'bag' of those field-grey forms. Ah! I'm glad I was on the side of those Inniskilling boys.

NOTHING ON THIS EARTH

See them crouched on the sunken road all night long, out in front of our own wire in no man's land, then, on that bright summer's morning of 1 July 1916 at the signal 'go', come to life and dash forward leading our attack on that supposedly 'untakeable' fortress on the slopes of Thiepval!

Were they denied? No! No! Nothing on God's earth could have stopped that wild Irish charge, and the Germans turned and fled. Could you blame them? I'm proud of my Regiment, but, by all the saints above me, I take off my hat to the Skins.

SNOWBOUND

A blinding snowstorm swept the countryside and all the world was white. It was impossible to see more than several yards ahead. We had just come down the line for a few days' rest. A fatigue party under my command was ordered to report at a little village some distance from our Battalion Headquarters. Our job was to unload a train of round timber logs.

SNOW! SNOW! SNOW!

Eventually we got there and worked all day in the snowflakes, and the cold. The task completed, we started out on our return journey as evening fell. The flakes were larger and thicker than ever; it was swirling around in ever increasing velocity and the snowdrifts were getting deeper and deeper.

WE ARE LOST

After struggling along for several hours, it dawned on us that we were lost and the night had now come down, but even if it had been daylight our plight would have been the same. A few feet ahead was just a wall of whirling, swirling snowflakes. Each step forward and we were sinking to the waist; our bodies were numb, hands were useless, and our strength was going, going slow for sure. We struggled on for hours, to get – nowhere! On! Ever on! But it was hopeless now. Round and round in circles we travelled; as we came across our tracks this awful fact struck us like a flash. We huddled together now for warmth and mutual support.

My nose was now bleeding, the red blood staining my greatcoat as it flowed down, turning to ice in a few minutes. What in God's name could we do? My men were at the point of exhaustion and collapse. They were hungry, cold, and miserable, poor fellows. Hour after hour sped by. There was no beauty in the snow now. How we raved and cursed. Our strength was surely giving out and the fatal desire to lie down came over me … Lie down and sleep, Jim! Just drop down! My brain was on fire – it hammered. Oh

LOST IN THE SNOW SEE STORY "SNOWBOUND"

how maddening it was! On! On! Boys! Keep moving or we perish. I urged, I cursed, I threatened them. Just a little longer lads, and we shall hit our camp. We battled on – here? The hours dragged on, it seemed like years to us. Not a living soul did we encounter. We fell down, rose up again, fell once more, and helped each other onward.

ARE WE TO DIE LIKE THIS?
My senses were going too. Here was I a sergeant in charge of the squad and we were all going to die in the snow! What a miserable end for soldiers who had come to France to fight the Germans.

GOD SAVE US – MY CRY!
A box of matches – yes! Gather round boys and warm your hands on a match. It was hopeless. Not one of us had the power to strike a light. Every match fell from our fingers and we were doomed – oh! God save us! Help us in our misery. This prayer was sent up by me as I hugged a chum who was almost on the verge of collapse.

ANSWERED?
Did Providence hear my prayer? Yes! To this day I feel convinced that it was answered as we staggered right into the midst of our camp a few minutes later. Just in time!

A whole evening and a night out in the snow. Our cup of sorrow was full and overflowing when we realised that during our absence our billet was flooded out and blankets soaked through and through. It's unforgettable!

THE VILLAGE CLOCK

MYSTERIOUS HANDS
Not all of us in this little town paid much attention to the movements of the clock on top of that old Town Hall.

Near enough to the firing line, it could be quite hot here at times and, as the district was a reserve line for weary troops, there was always a great deal of movement in the village.

We did notice that Jerry took delight in sending over a perfect hail of shells at times, mostly when we were moving up to the front-line trenches.

GONE! WHERE!
One fine morning the 'hands' were gone – clean off. How could that have happened? A mystery! Yes! Very mysterious.

TO IRELAND
Many weary years afterwards we were told the story of those 'hands' at one of our Battalion reunions by our captain and Adjutant, Captain Mulholland.

THE VILLAGE CLOCK

A TRUE STORY OF THE WAR

STEEPLEJACK OFFICERS
This clock caused much comment amongst our officers by its irregular time keeping; the hands often jumped at an alarming speed, and when they did we always got a 'strafe' from the enemy guns.

Worth looking into! What?

Plans were laid; one dark night, by a supreme act of steeplejack work on the part of our officers, that spire was scaled and the hands removed. These found their way back to Ireland and, long after the war was over, figured in a social event in that little town in northern France when a party of the 14th Royal Irish Rifles were received in great pomp by the Mayor and the population to receive the 'missing hands'. This was all that had been left of that Town Hall after four and a half years of war.

A VILLAGE TREASURE
They now rest in the new Town Hall, a treasure for ever and for all time.

A TRAITOR AT WORK?
It was a spy, or traitor, that had been working them, the signal being taken up by the German artillery observation post and this, no doubt, was the explanation for the many fierce bombardments that swept over us as we moved in or out to this next village.

That is the story of the village clock.

MY LITTLE RAT

THIS spell in the line stands out in my memory – I made a strange friend.

FORGOT ABOUT WAR
Soaked through, tired and covered with slime I dragged my weary body back a few yards down the communication trench and crawled into my dug-out to rest for a few hours. Throwing myself down, it was only a few minutes before I had forgotten all about the mud, bully beef, and war, and was sound asleep. On duty always, my equipment was still fixed on and the iron rations (reserve food) were in my haversack.

SETTING OUT SUPPER
When I woke up I was amazed to find that this said haversack had been eaten through (a tough job) and one of my nice army biscuits all nibbled away. Surely this little beggar was hungry? More amused than angry, I made up my mind to test the little fellow next night, so I set a biscuit outside on my overcoat, and then fell asleep.

HE FELL FOR IT
Did he turn up? He certainly did! And what's more he had his food, then calmly crawled inside my greatcoat, snugged himself up, and then fell asleep too, right on my chest! Can you credit it?

TOMMY ROONEY KNOCKED OUT
McClay and Joe Johnston milked them! At least they tried to and the result was not encouraging, so it was again voted that two different lads should have a shot at it. Rooney and Rogers then had a go and Tommy Rooney nearly lost his life – from a backhanded kick. He was finished, and so was our milk!

We handed them over to our relief, the Skins.

THE NIGHT PATROL

STRAIGHT DOWN THE MUZZLE WE LOOKED!

A MACHINE-GUN NEST had been giving us a great deal of trouble. Orders from HQ had been received to send out a patrol and if possible to locate it (at night). My old friend Mr Wedgewood, platoon officer of No.15 Platoon informed me during the day and asked me to accompany him on his venture. Would I go?

Sure and I'm delighted Sir, answered myself! Then we took stock. Good strong field-glasses were brought into play, no man's land examined, and the route mapped out for tonight's work.

A STAGE SCENE
12.30pm that night witnessed a very strange scene. In the little dug-out we met. Off came all our badges, numerals, and tell-tale marks. Faces were then blackened, papers, letters etc. were thrown out from our pockets. Big six-shooters oiled, cleaned, and loaded up. Several Mills bombs stuffed into the empty pockets – and we were ready.

A WARNING
A dark wet miserable night as we crawled through our wire, after giving the word to our sentries – not to do any shooting – and watch for our return.

RAILWAY IN NO MAN'S LAND
Our objective was at an angle, on an embankment of the railway line that ran through our lines out into the German lines through no man's land, the distance across being some one hundred and fifty yards.

UNBURIED ... BUT UNTROUBLED
Getting low down we soon cleared our own barbed wire and started to crawl along the dark, damp wet ground.

Shell hole to shell hole we moved on. Gee! What a smell here, in one of these; was it some unburied soul that had lain for – but neither cold nor heat troubles him anymore. We passed at our best speed. A star shell lights up the heavens. We sit in our tracks – and imagine ourselves as large as – as large as the City Hall, Belfast.

PING! PING! ZIP !ZIP!
Ping! Ping! Zip! Zip! Those blasted bullets zipped around and over us. We paid little or no attention to them as the business on hand was important. No time to lose – dodging bullets.

WHAT AN AGE
Pitch dark, direction was difficult. We kept close together for safety and comradeship. An hour or so must have now passed. Surely our destination was round about here?

BRIGHT AS DAY
Heavens above! What a flash! Spell-bound, I was rooted to the spot, could not move a finger even! It burst right behind us … that awful star shell … brighter than daylight … and we lay revealed – what a sight met our gaze … straight down the muzzle we looked, and the gun crew just as incapable of movement as ourselves.

Not a shadow of doubt about it. We had struck the spot, and with a vengeance too! Not ten yards away. Action came to us first and we literally threw ourselves over the side of the embankment to plunge down – down – down – to what? The gun flashes start the darkness. Rat tat – tat – tat, tat – tat! But the target had gone.

A BOLT FROM ABOVE
A wild tumble, head over heels, and we were shot to the bottom of the slope. We struck them like a bolt from the sky itself – a new form of shell, or bomb! Yes!, right into the midst of a German patrol we landed. They neither knew nor could they see what had struck them.

Guttural oaths, shouts and a wild stampede, they bolted like mad, scattering in all directions, down the railway track, and so did we. Gasping for breath, it slowly dawned on us how near we had been to death – and perhaps worse, capture – as we clutched each other by the arm to scale that steep slope again and get clear of the railway line below.

STILL SPLUTTERING
Blast that d***** machine gun. It was still barking, and spluttering as we veered in towards our lines to eventually drop into our own front-line trench, all bruised, cut, and tore into ribbons but safe!

BIG STARING EYES
What an adventure, all crowded into an hour or so. Yet it seemed like years. I'm looking down that grim steel barrel yet, and those figures crouching behind it – big eyes staring at us in bewilderment.

RESULTS
Our information gave the artillery a line of fire. Result? A little peace.

PICTURES.~ THE NIGHT PATROL ~

Drawn in Hospital 1916.

ADVENTURE

TRENCH WARFARE ON THE SOMME 1915-16

RAIN – mud – snow and filth … then more … everywhere!
What misery! Day and night we lived in it. Winter days are still with us – and a long dreary one it has been – but our spirits never failed; we were always on the lookout for that 'silver lining' that the song told us about.

The rifle was just covered with mud and about as much use as a walking stick – at times. Greatcoats were cut short, at the bottom, to take away that awful driving down feeling. How we existed the Lord only knows, as our bones were chilled to the marrow. Our feet! Had we any? Body and soul was wearied out, dragging our bodies through that awful slime, often up to our waist, and over.

NO RELIEF
The little shelters afforded little or no relief. They had a foot or so of evil-smelling filth as a floor; you just sat, or threw yourself down, into it! Even the old battered coke braziers give out no heat. We could not get warm – still we battled on!

A thousand – yes! a million, times worse than an attack. Could they not send us over? But then, old Jerry was perhaps as badly off as us. Would our blood never warm?

SIMPLY TORTURE
Bringing up the rations was one long march of torture. Step by step, yard by yard, we crawled back for our big churn of tea or hot soup – and the return journey was fifty times worse. Then the food was cold when it reached the troops. But what more could we do?

TO KEEP US WARM?
The Huns sent over a few shells to keep us alive. It was a hopeless job rebuilding trenches and dug-outs.

UP WITH THE SOUP.

ALMOST ENVIED HIM

Sometimes a little party wended their way back – back behind the lines – to lay a comrade to rest, rest from it all, and sometimes we almost envied him, that chum of ours.

CANNOT BE TOLD

Seven or eight days of this then back – back to all of it – again! After a rest in billets. Misery that cannot be told.

THE WEE SHOP

DID YOU SEE HER, SERGEANT?
14 PLATOON was all excitement. One of the boys whispered, 'Did you see her Sergeant?' 'See who?' I replied! 'Ah! She's a whopper! Down below in the "wee shop".' Naturally I had to see this beauty, so down I popped and made a purchase. Yes! She was a fine big strapping lass, a real blonde, but I noticed she did not display her hands a great deal. She was painted up! Slapped on like a circus turn. For all that, the boys agreed she was not half bad looking, and that little shop got a fine run of trade from No.14 Platoon. But one fine morning it was a case of shutters up and the 'wee shop' was napoo. Oh where, oh where, had our little bird gone?

WE NEVER KNEW
No one knew, or ever found out, so far as I knew, but the story goes that 'she' was a German spy, all dressed up as a French Lassie and 'she' was a 'man'. What nerve! Right in the midst of the British troops, selling us postcards, chocolates, wine, etc.

THE FIRING SQUAD?
They took her away – away to what, a fate we knew that befell all spies – the firing squad? But 'she' was brave, and deserved a better fate.

French detectives, or secret military police pounced on him and 'come along, please' was the command! This was the yarn that went the rounds, and believe me there was 'something' in it.

STOLEN HEARTS
Now the funny part of it all was that some of our dashing young lady killers actually lost their heads and hearts to this fair charmer, and that was a sore point amongst them when we raked up the past and mentioned this blonde. Of course, I should not tell this part of the story as some of our Irish sweethearts and wives may wonder!

SOUVENIR
It may interest you to know that the picture on opposite page was actually bought in the 'wee shop' and has since been treasured by me.

WHAT IT LOOKED LIKE.

ESTAMINET

Jim Maultsaid — 1917

THE WEE SHOP

PICTURE WAS BOUGHT IN THE WEE SHOP BY

Jim Maultsaid

1917.

THEY FELL FOR HER!

Star Shell Reflections 1914–1916

GONE TO THE DOGS

GONE TO~THE DOGS

WEARY
WE STAGGERED IN

MY EYE CAUGHT SIGHT OF A BIG DOG BOX.

~ HE WAS IN HIS BOX ~

FAST ASLEEP.

PICTURES
~ BY ~
Jim. MAULTSAID

FOR A NIGHT

TIRED OUT AND WEARY WE STAGGERED IN
After some twenty five kilos of footslogging in the rain and through the mud, we arrived at our rest billets for the night. The usual routine of stores, blankets etc. being duly unloaded we were by this time dropping off our feet with exhaustion. The problem of housing the troops was acute.

My lot was an unhappy one, as I found myself in the air, so to speak, after pushing the last man of my platoon in somehow. It was my duty to see my platoon all 'snugged in', and now I was 'left'.

Not a spot could I find. This was a mess. Casting my eye around, it fell on a huge dog kennel – and a big dog as occupier. Clean straw, looked inviting, so I plucked up courage and with soft words plus an army biscuit I made overtures. He was friendly, thank goodness, so I just crawled inside the box and slept the night through, undisturbed, but it was a shock to wake up in the early hours of the morning, and find my head resting on the side of a big dog. He got a good breakfast – and we parted firm friends.

SIDELIGHTS
ALL the way through my army career I took a deep interest in my chums, in my surroundings, and noted the humorous incidents in writing or by a simple little sketch (in the rough) and then completed the drawings when the first opportunity presented itself.

BY SKETCH AND STORY
YOU may now study these yourself as they present themselves in this book. Most are from real life – and better still I took part in almost all of them myself, so therefore you are getting a true insight into the life we boys led during those fateful years 1914 to 1918 when the world was upside down and we young men were thrown into the furnace of war, facing death, wounds or disease, day and daily, yet holding to life – and cheerfully enduring the hardship that befell us on our travels.

YOU ARE THE JUDGE
MY modest claim that no better war book has ever been put together – and nothing fairer ever written – is an honest boast. YOU are the Judge.

SIDELIGHTS
HOME SWEET HOME
DEMMOBED?
BELFAST TELEGRAPH
"EYES RIGHT
THEIR BATTLES OVER
- AGAIN -
ANGRY SERGT (TO RECRUIT) YOU ARE THE BIGGEST MUFF
RECRUIT - YES SEGT !
TO KEEP YOU WARM.
A FEW SUGGESTIONS FOR THE
- NEXT WAR -
SUNSHINE TRENCH
NO MORE MUD.
NO FIGHTING FROM 4 P. M. TILL 9. A.M.
A STAINLESS RUSTLESS & UNCLEANABLE RIFLE
NO SUNDAY FIGHTING
RUBBER BULLETS.
SHAVE WHEN YOU LIKE.
IN FACT
LIVE & LET LIVE

FEEDING THE GUNS.

JIM. MAULTSAID
25th. DEC. 1916.

THE GIRL BEHIND THE GUNS.

HEAVY ARTILLERY IN ACTION

BIG RAILWAY GUN FIRING

SHELLING THE ZEP'S

THE MULE CARRIER

ALL DRAWN BY

JIM. MAULTSAID

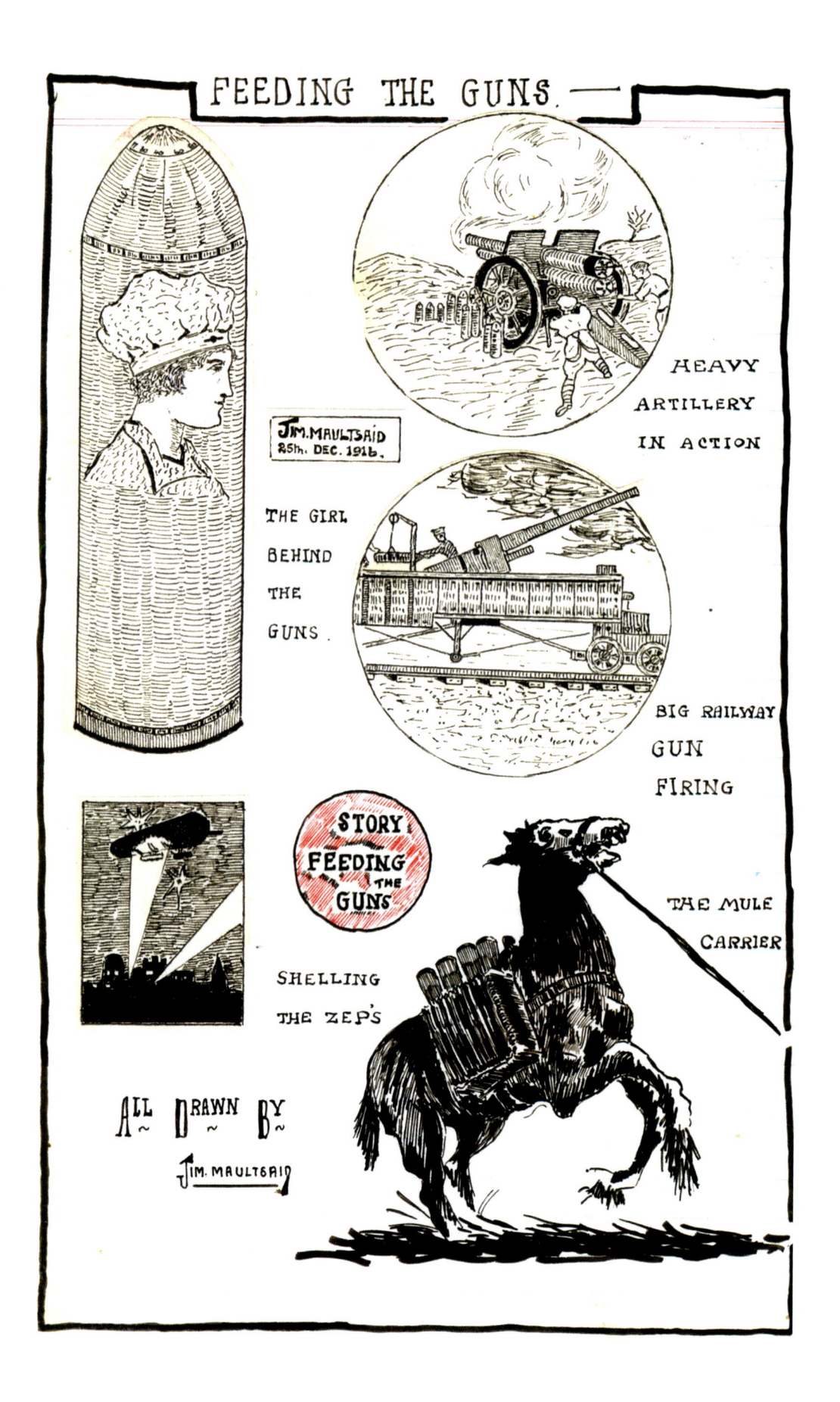

FEEDING THE GUNS

THEY WERE NEVER SATISFIED

IN the days before such things as labour battalions were known, the PBI (poor bloody infantrymen) were turned to all kinds of jobs, as you will no doubt have already observed from the pages gone before. These jobs were considered as 'rest'; we performed them when out on our seven days or so from the line, so you see what 'Tommy' had to put up with in 1914, 1915 and 1916! Feeding ourselves was quite bad enough, but feeding the hungry guns was worse. Big shells that took several of us to handle, small ones that you could have thrown around like skittles and the in between sizes, all came under our loving care. Ah! It was a great life! Just drop one – and no more worries on this old earth, but we were careful enough.

All kinds of stunts were used to get the 'dope' up to the gunpits, such as light railways, mules, limbers and manpower – that's wee us and co.

GIVE THE PBI A PAIN

Night-time was the favourite hour to get the news that so many of the troops were required to report at 'hell-blast' avenue for fatigue. Here you are, Sergeant. These trucks must be pushed right up to - - - - - then come back here for more! Understand? Yes! I d*** well do! And what a night for the job. Those wee trucks weighed something when we had them loaded up with big 5.9-inch shells. Did the gunners keep us to unload? Not much! To see them direct us from a big warm dug-out, and it raining as if the heavens would burst gave us a pain, and we did not miss telling them a few things about guns and gunners too! Of course, the gun crews were really good fellows; only we had to have our grouse.

PACK MULES

The mules came in useful. To see them toil through the mud with their creels strapped on each side, just like the old Irish donkey bringing in the turf, only not to this time but tubes of death and destruction. Shells! Shells! Shells!

BOTTLE PRACTICE

NO, my friend you are wrong! It was not a practice on how to empty bottles – but how to break them by sharpshooting!

GREAT FUN FOR 14 PLATOON
You can see them all in a row above. This was a favourite pastime of mine and 14 Platoon enjoyed it. Also it was making the boys all crack shots, so it was a game with the real purpose.

FIVE FRANCS THE WINNER
Several of the boys made a tour of the village beer shops and collected all the bottles that could be procured. These were generally all colours from red to yellow, and blue. Then away we went, out to the country, and selected a background that would stop all our bullets. Two stakes were driven in some twenty yards apart, and wire stretched out, then the bottles tied on a foot apart. Rapid fire – five francs to the winner – and the bottles 'napoo'.

D COMPANY ... UP A TREE

FALL OUT ... D COMPANY
At the bottom of a hill we rested. The old pack straps were loosened, we flung ourselves down for a few minutes. The going had been hard, very hard; we were tired and sore.

RIGHT ABOVE US
Along the road on each side of us (the famous D Company) big apple trees hung over and nice red apples hung above our heads; just imagine the temptation! Could we stick it? Troops are troops, and this was D Company, so, of course, no apples – this was the order anyhow!

A ONE MAN COMPANY!
Rodgers could stand it no longer. He was through the bushes like a shadow and in no time delivered the goods. Nice red, plump apples showered down and the rush was like a rugby scrum.

STILL A GOOD JOKE
The hubbub attracted Captain Willis, and he yelled, 'D Company. Come down that tree.' D Company was Rogers.

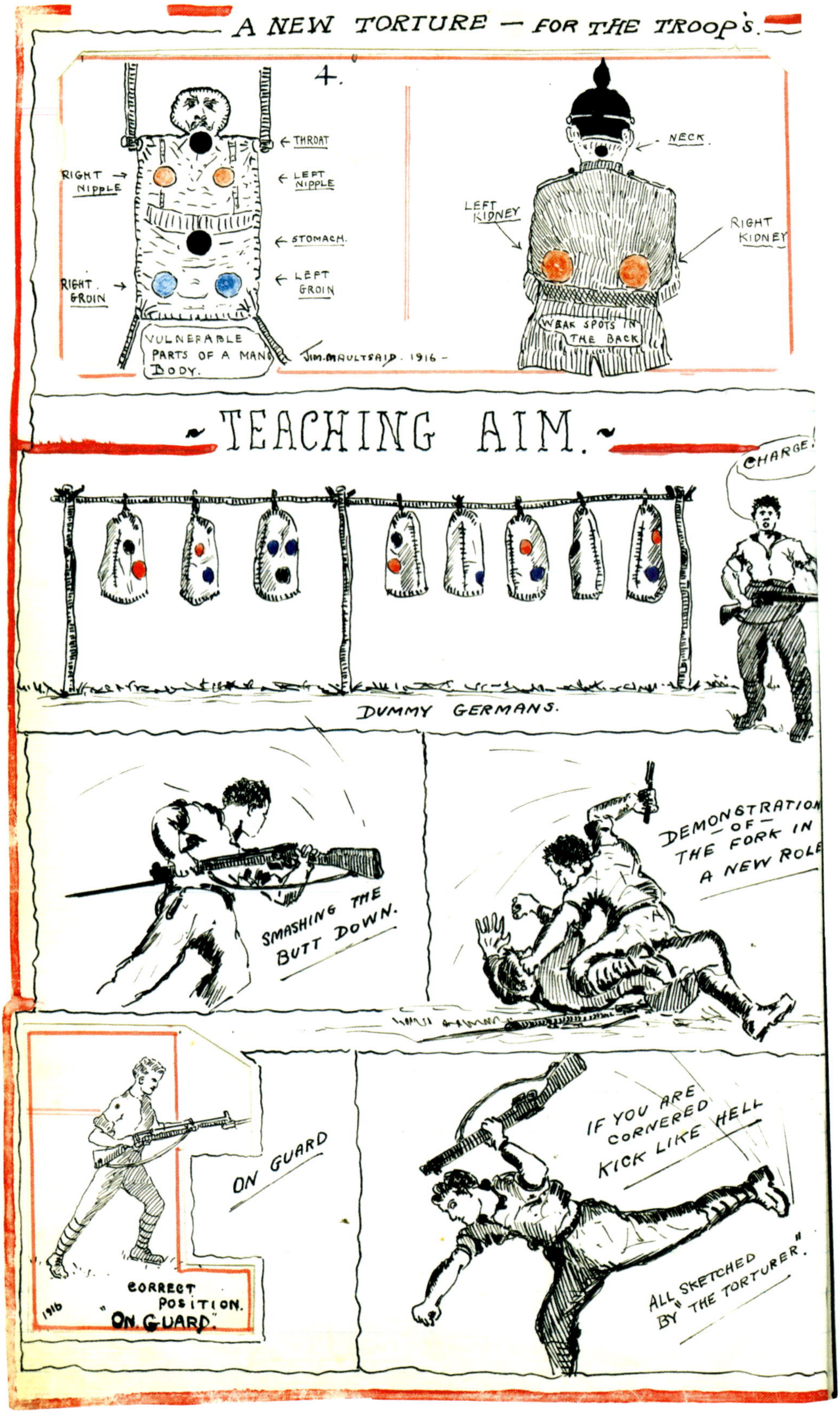
A NEW TORTURE – FOR THE TROOP'S.
4.
THROAT
RIGHT NIPPLE
LEFT NIPPLE
STOMACH.
RIGHT. GROIN
LEFT GROIN
VULNERABLE PARTS OF A MANS BODY.
JIM. MAULTSAID. 1916.
NECK.
LEFT KIDNEY
RIGHT KIDNEY
WEAK SPOTS IN THE BACK
TEACHING AIM.
CHARGE!
DUMMY GERMANS.
SMASHING THE BUTT DOWN.
DEMONSTRATION – OF – THE FORK IN A NEW ROLE
ON GUARD
CORRECT POSITION. "ON GUARD"
1916
IF YOU ARE CORNERED KICK LIKE HELL
ALL SKETCHED BY "THE TORTURER".

A NEW TORTURE

INVENTED BY ME FOR THE TROOPS

I had been through a school of instruction for bayonet fighting. Arriving back with my Battalion I had in the meantime put in some deep thinking and drawn up a new programme of 'torture for the troops'.

A FINE MIXTURE

My idea was to combine physical culture, sport, rough horseplay, and bayonet exercises altogether. A solid hour's going – all out, with a few short breaks for a lungful of fresh air. This was to be tried out on my own unfortunate platoon. Of course, I had to get my platoon officer's authority. No difficulty here as Lieutenant Monard was an out-and-out sport and, of course, he wanted his boys to be 'it' in the bayonet department.

'Can you do it, Maultsaid?' 'Sure I can, Sir. Just let me try!'

'No. 14 Platoon! Fall in! Jackets off! Sleeves up! Tighten your belts now! I'm off. A short demonstration of how to take good deep breath! You'll need it all in a few minutes. Watch me carefully.' Grasping my rifle and bayonet I went through several strange movements. The squad were put through the same business. Ground arms! Get ready to sprint. 'See yon sacks hanging on the pales?' 'Yes!'

'There and back like h*** Go!'

'Take a rest now. On the back, down. Legs up. One two, one two. Get up! Mark time! Double mark time! Come on; faster, faster. Lift 'em up. Stand easy. Take note.'

I smash into an imaginary opponent with the butt end of my rifle. I parry, I lunge – swifter and swifter my movements become until I have worked myself into a perfect tornado of arms, legs and the bayonets. 'By G**,' whispers one of the lads, 'what in h***'s name is this?'

'You bite, you kick, get him anywhere – but get him first! Do you all get me? Let's see you try.'

They go through the mill. 'Not fast enough, try again. Come along! Speed up!'

Quicker and quicker they whirl around. All for speed, and punch.

'Sit down and take an eyeful of your dear little sergeant, please.'

They rest again. 'Quite simple! What? Yes! I can take the rifle and bayonet from my opponent. Impossible you say? Come out here, Savage, and I'll show you how it's done.'

Savage advances – at the attack. I dodge, grasp his rifle as he blunders past, throw it down, grasp him – and lo! he is on his back, unarmed. I take out my fork from the top of my puttee and make an imaginary stab at his throat. He turns pale. Get up my lad, you're dead.' (Irish what?)

By this time most of my platoon either believe in me, or put me down as being mad. I'm far from that.

Just full of life – and pep!

AN IRISH CHARGE
'Fall in! Get ready to charge! Listen now. No dog trot this! Full speed ahead. Take those sacks fifty yards away as your enemy and when I say go! Go like blazes. All ready? Go!'

A mad whirling mob surges forward, and take the dummy sacks by storm. Good work well done. How could any enemy face that bunch of Irish lads.

I CUT OUT PARADE STUFF
All parade ground stuff was cut clean out. It was a free and easy bit of training. My idea was full control of the squad and train them in my own way.

Lieutenant Monard was indeed pleased, so pleased was he that I had a special call to demonstrate my system that evening to all the battalion officers. Just imagine! My squad were one and two star men, and by the holy smoke I put them through it with a vengeance.

Ah! It was great stuff!

My fame spread like a flame.

DEMONSTRATIONS
Each afternoon it was a request to Lieutenant Monard for the loan of Sergeant Maultsaid for A Company, and for B Company and for C Company. Right round the lot.

TO GET ME?
One gent made up his mind to get me. He tried. And failed. Yes! It's true, you can read it all in the printed article entitled 'The spirit of the bayonet' by J. B. O'Neill on the previous page. This article was written about me and my system.

FIT AS FIDDLES
Never were men so fit; and never did I enjoy myself more. But the call for the trenches came and we moved up the line once more.

SWAMP LIFE

LIVING IN WATER …

UP TO THE WAIST

RIGHT up to the waist in ice-cold water, our new part of the line was a swamp and we lived like water rats. Day in, day out, same at night, no getting away from it; the one and only good point was that mud was scarcer, and the water was cleaner.

FRONT LINE IN A SWAMP
OUR line faced 'Jerry' through this swamp and of course it had to be held, so little outposts were formed on the bits of firm ground. Rough barricades of sandbags, tree trunks, and rubbish were thrown up for protection (?), then two or three men manned

– SWAMP LIFE –

Jim Maultsaid. From a rough original pencil sketch 1916.
— 1917 —

Jim. Maultsaid. 1917.
Re sketched from from a pencil original drawn "on the spot" in 1916 –

the defence. You had to lie stretched out on your stomach, with the black water swirling around your feet. Living like water fowl in a world of water, tree stumps and silence that was only broken by the cry of a wild bird, or the splash of a German shell as it ploughed its way into the soft earth to send up a huge waterspout. There were hundreds of shells that never exploded thrown at us, and that old swamp must indeed be a regular scrap iron dump to this day.

A WATERY GRAVE

DUTIES were so severe on the troops that shorter spells and quicker relief was the order. It was a nightmare getting out to these little posts. It was my business to visit them once a day, and during the night. Stumbling, slipping into a deep evil-looking pool that pulled you down! Down! Right up to the armpits, grasping the bank grass to save yourself from drowning, then crawling out, to blunder on through the darkness, sense of direction lost, just trusting to luck and the flash of enemy star shells away up behind Thiepval, or in front of Beaumont Hamel. God! It was a grizzly experience this, these night-time trips out to the pure wretches holding the line.

The story was told that this was no natural swamp, but it was made by the French early in the war as a barrier and it was certainly all that as no troops could have attacked through this death-trap sector – in the winter time anyhow. The little river Ancre, a tributary of the Somme, flowed through this forest swamp, but its banks were all destroyed by shell fire etc., and the water just flowed anywhere.

DO YOU TAKE US FOR NAVY MEN?

TEN long days and nights of this water rat existence, in the dead of winter would try the best troops in the world. We stuck it of course as we were good soldiers; but for all that we were glad to see our old friends the Inniskillings turn up one wet winter's night and take over from us.

Some fun in the handing of our care to the Skins. They asked us 'where are the boats?' And was it rough at sea? Did we take them for Navy men? Etc., etc.
109 BRIGADE SHOULD LONG REMEMBER 'THAT SWAMP'.

THE FIERY FURNACE

WINTER days have almost passed away and the songbirds fill the air. Trees have taken on a new brown colour, the earth smells sweet. Conditions underfoot have improved; the old enemy, mud, has dried up and life is again worth living. We cast aside our goatskin coats, the extra blanket has been returned to the Quarter Master's store. There is new vitality in the air, and the troops take new heart. Thank God to be alive! And my health is fine. Never was I so fit and well as in these spring days.

The YCVs had carried out every order, and all our allotted duties in a fine soldier-like manner.

Hardships had been met, and overcome; long days of misery gone through, days of want – days too of hunger – when I shared my little white loaf into sixteen equal parts and not a

A FIERY FURNACE

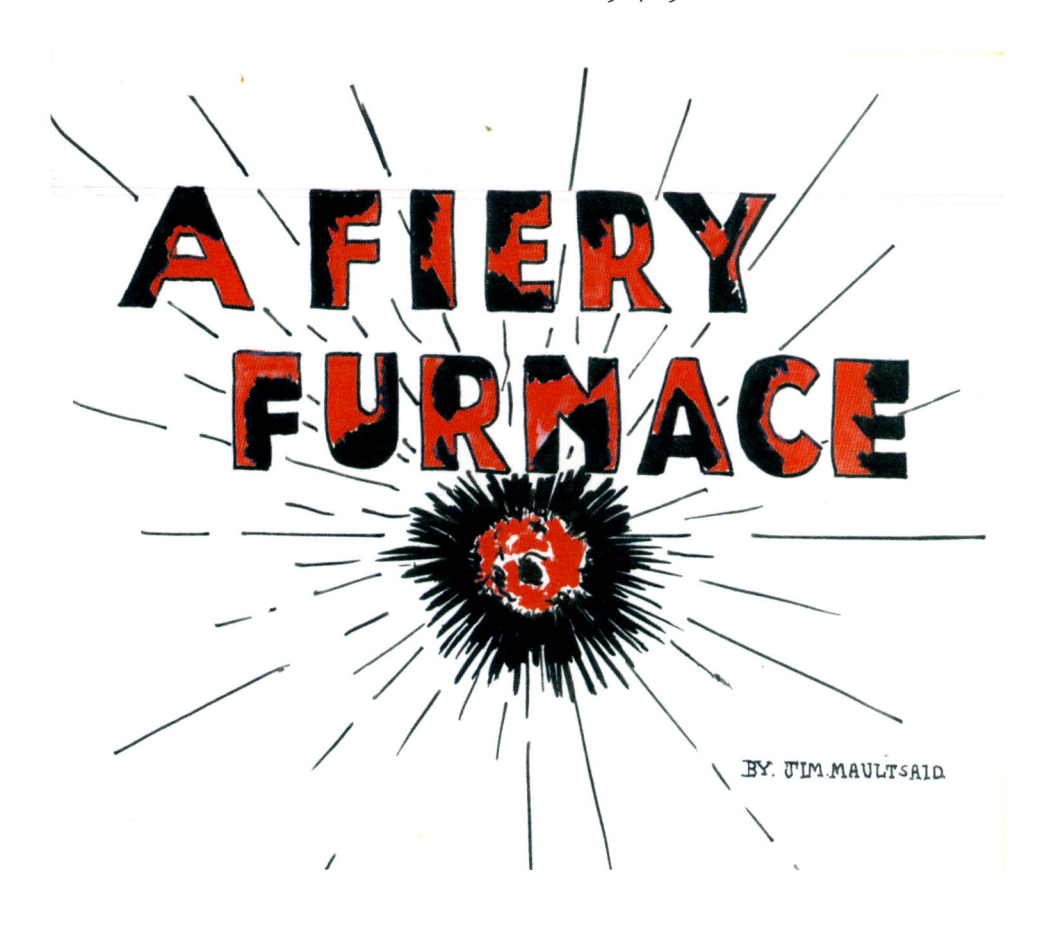

BY JIM MAULTSAID

scrap even left for myself! Yes! Reader it's true; my beloved platoon came first and I often brought my belt a bit tighter to keep the feeling of want from my stomach pit! All for the boys. But oh! They were great lads, those lads of No. 14.

We had taken our place in the line, again and again. We had covered hundreds of weary miles, through the shell-shattered villages of France, and were now a seasoned battalion of hard-bitten, hard fighting Irishmen! Scores of our chums had gone, some forever and some back to England with wounds, wounds that would take years and years to heal, but we who were left to carry on the good work kept our hearts up and just 'carried on'.

Now the song of spring was in the air. Gone were the dull dark days of winter … and we still lived!

Back once more, manning the front-line trenches, waiting watching 'Jerry'. Always on the alert day and night; little sleep, no rest practically – you stood up and dozed, when off duty. It was a lively front now.

Shellfire. Big Black Berthas that came out of the sky like an express train to crash down amongst the earthworks and send us staggering with the shock and sickening fumes. A rush, duck down. Crouch – and wait!

It certainly was not – ALL QUIET NOW, ON THIS FRONT.

AT THE HEIGHT OF THE STORM

Sketch by Tim Maultsaid

A Fiery Furnace. "Pictures."

Gone are the days of eternal mud

New life was everywhere — The song of spring in the air!

1 white loaf into 16 parts — and none for myself.

The old belt was brought tighter.

Hundreds of weary miles covered through shell shattered villages.

We had slept standing up.

Up the line again

Helping a pal back to the dressing station.

A rush — duck down, crouch and wait!

Watching! Waiting!

Stand to! Dashing up the communication trench to the firing line.

ALL FROM MY FIELD SKETCH BOOK.

Night had fallen. Dark and cold, but dry. The date was 6 April 1916. The quietness of the line disturbed us a little, we always suspected something from across the way. Experience had taught us that, and we were more keyed up than usual. Why? Just suspicion I suppose. Anyhow my little black book reads: 'Our battalion passed through a fierce bombardment with great credit 6/4/16.'

CRASH! BANG! Faster and still faster they came. The roar, and the rattle, was deafening! Blue, red, green rockets soared up from the German lines! My! He had the wind up tonight – and by G★★ he was letting us have it, right in the neck. Shells were bursting all around us. The barbed-wire defences were being smashed to atoms. The trenches were falling in – the ground was heaving and swaying.

Stand to! Stand to!

Man the front line. See the figures scurrying up to their positions. Faces that looked green – a funny green too! Looked up from beneath the 'tin hats'; hands grasped the rifles, loaded up – and then waited! Waited! Waited! Would he attack? Let him come! Better, a thousand times, a fight, than this – standing being blown to bits. Our guns took up the challenge. What a din. Cr-a-s-h! One could almost picture the shells crossing each other in no man's land. The gun duel raged for hours, and the wee brown khaki figures clung to their trenches. Not a yard did we retreat, and we weathered the biggest storm of our career – so far!

Well done, the 14th Royal Irish Rifles (YCV).

I LOSE A PAL

I LOSE A PAL
"BILLY"! HE HAS GONE!

BILLY! HE HAS GONE!

They told me next morning. He died firing his machine gun. All that was found of him was his right hand clasping the trigger of his beloved gun. Blown to bits – was poor Willie Reid. That old red head would dodge my punches no more (we often had a few rounds with the gloves). No more would I share my little parcels from home with him. Somehow this was my greatest blow – so far – and now nevermore would I see him! Ah! It was hard. But Billy boy I lived to revenge your death – and I did not forget! Old pal of mine.

That night of 6 April 1916 is still a memory of mine. And when they carried all the mortal remains of you Willie, wrapped up in a blanket and sandbag back behind the lines to rest in that old French graveyard, a little of me went down with you!

THE INCINERATOR

'IT WAS HOT'

OURS – AND FOR US – YES!

HOW THE TROOPS ENJOYED IT. Yes, it was like a ray of sunshine in our drab lives, this little magazine of ours! We owe Lieutenant Monard a great debt, for the thought, and the actual carrying out, of this great work.

Working under difficulties he accomplished a magnificent piece of work in producing this Battalion magazine whilst in active service. I sincerely hope that copies are filed in the British War Museum to show what could be done, and was done, by the 14th Royal Irish Rifles (YCV) during the Great War 1914-18.

I have great pleasure of knowing that I assisted in this work. This was a job just after my own heart, and my little sketches, also articles, helped to keep the flag flying. You may read some of the choice gems from our 'our Mag' on the following pages – and enjoy them.

The name of the magazine means 'burning rubbish' in one of our homemade destructions, but it was far from being 'rubbish'. It was a masterpiece! It breathed the spirit of the troops – that spirit (not rum or vin-blong) that carried us to the Rhine in 1918.

THE EDITOR OF THAT FAMOUS PAPER

THE INCINERATOR

LIEUTENANT S. H. MONARD

WE did not understand him at first and somehow no matter how we tried, our efforts were not satisfactory. He was hard, yes very hard, to please, but, looking back, I can now see it was all for our own good: he just wanted No. 14 Platoon to be 'it'. To my mind he was a far better active service officer than a home one.

From the day we landed in France he was a new man, and a great officer. Nothing was too much, or too great a trouble, if it was for the benefit of his beloved platoon.

He was hard to bluff, and had no time for scroungers, but was fair in his judgement. A man for sport of all kind, he was a fine athlete himself; he encouraged us to go in for all sporting events and loved to see us win, all for D Company.

WHY AN IRISH REGIMENT?

A Londoner by birth, I never found out his reasons for joining an 'Irish mob', but I do know he grew to love us, 'his Irish troops'. He possessed a keen sense of humour. I know he thoroughly enjoyed our little ways, and had many a laugh at our antics. I can see him yet laughing at the 'Dixie kid' when he popped out as twelfth man in the D Company football team, and would hardly go off.

A GREAT FIGHTER

As a leader of men, as a fighter, yes! Lieutenant Monard was a man, and I had supreme faith in him. We fought side-by-side on that mighty day 1 July 1916 – and by G** he could fight!

If ever a decoration was earned, he sure did earn one for bravery. Yet, so far as I know, he never received one. Such is life. Such things did not worry him. He was too much of a gentleman.

MY PRIVILEGE

It was my privilege to serve under him in the Great War, and still to count on him as a great friend after all these years.

FOOTNOTE

It was my great privilege to take part in the getting together of secret information (in the sporting end only) to write short paragraphs, to make little black and white sketches, to suggest headings for the various articles and assist generally behind the scenes in producing this mag of ours.

My platoon officer and editor made the discovery that I was more or less a past master in this line. By the way I was an editor myself in my school days and produced a little amateur mag called *The Emerald* that eventually simply overwhelmed me by the circulation leaping into thousands of copies, so you can see how much I was in my natural element in helping to run our Battalion Magazine.

Unfortunately, I cannot show you many copies of our little paper, as in the hectic days in France it was impossible to keep these for future historians, but what you have seen in the previous pages should convince you that it was simply first class and a marvellous production when on active service.

THE DIXIE KID – A STAR TURN

A PRODUCT OF D COMPANY

AS I remarked on the other pages, we, the famous D Company, had some 'rare cards' on the strength.

'The Dixie kid' was one of them. He got his name, I think, owing to his fondness for that old army 'essential', the dixie lid, especially when there was dip bread on it, and some bacon.

A HUMAN MACHINE GUN

How he dodged into the army is far beyond me. But there he was – and one of my flock, too! Father of thirteen children, his place was at home, helping to look after them! What say you? Yet we find him mixing it with the rest of us, and keeping his end up too! Oh! He was a lad! An incessant grouse. No one paid the least notice to him; he just rumbled on, and on. A human machine gun that never ran short of ammunition. To hear him in a battle of wits with Father McBride and Porky Black was as good a turn as one could ever wish to hear – and he did not always lose!

A stout heart indeed did beat under the old khaki tunic, and his little short legs covered the lonesome miles just as well as ours. That little moustache hid the pain of winter days in the trenches, and he lived to grouse.

A PEST AT THE QM's STORE

Game for anything, he would parade at the Quarter Master's store and make a request for extra blankets, or extra anything, and get the 'hammer' for his pains. Was he disheartened? No! He just tried again.

A SURE STARTER

His name was entered for the battalion sports. He was warned a few hours before the event, and you find him amongst the starters. Down on the list as a boxer; the orderly sergeant read out 'Dixie kid' in the nine-stone division, and again he popped up. Pluck! Yes! Full of it, and then some!

A JOKE THAT ALMOST CAME OFF

He nearly played football for D Company. We were to meet the old rivals, the stage was set. I had warned Dixie he was picked as outside right the night previous. Hundreds and hundreds of 'fans' lined the touchline. Here comes D Company, and 'the kid' trots out also. His pants were cut down (a good pair of khaki longs had been sacrificed); he made twelve players. What a roar he got. It took us all our time to get him removed.

Let me introduce you to... THE DIXIE KID.

His fondness for "DIP" was well known

FATHER OF 13

"OLD BILL" HAD NOTHING ON OUR "DIXIE KID"

THOSE SHORT STUMPY LEGS COULD COVER THE LONESOME MILES AS WELL AS THE BEST OF US

QUARTER MASTERS STORE
NO ADMITTANCE

Would chance his arm at the Q.M's Store

IN THE 9 STONE DIVISION

CUT DOWNS! GOOD PANTS SACRIFICED

ALMOST GOT HIS CAP FOR D COMPANY

WHEN HE TURNED UP AS "TWELTH" MAN IT NEARLY CAUSED A RIOT

Jim. Maultsaid

OUR GOAT SMUGGLED IN

BORN in Randalstown, this mascot became attached to the battalion and took up quarters officially with the transport. As a mere youngster it was smuggled on board the big transport ship down at Southampton (in a limber wagon) and duly landed in France with the troops to share our joys and sorrows in that foreign land.

LIKED THE MUSIC

How rapidly it grew up! In a very short space of time it was a fully-fledged 'Billy Goat'. A fine specimen too, and in due course it got so wise that it could take its place at the head of the battalion – up beside the band. Ah! That goat loved music. How it dashed up the moment the band struck up, almost knocking some of the boys down in its wild rush. Or was it swank and vanity, to be at the top of the affairs?

BRASS HATS SHOCKED

Survivors of our lot can surely bring to mind one fine day when 109 Brigade was being reviewed by the 'red-hats' and the 14th Rifles were marching past when, like a bolt from the blue, our mascot came dashing through the ranks of the Inniskillings and proudly placed itself in front of its 'own' Battalion. What a shock for the staff! But the troops enjoyed it thoroughly. So did 'Billy the Goat'. He had actually escaped from captivity to take part in this ground dress parade.

DANCED WITH JOY

Or again, who can forget his great joy when his lord and master came back from leave? Reader! You can believe me or not, but that goat walked down the street of that old French town – on his hind legs – prancing like a thoroughbred horse full of delight and joy at getting his master back once more.

HOW DID HE END UP?

How did 'Billy' end his days? Sorry to say I cannot tell you, but he certainly acted his part in the Great War.

BOMBED FROM THE AIR

Our Battalion lay in a little old French town, the seven days in the line just over and we were settling down for some very necessary rest.

TERROR FROM THE SKY

Down! Down! He zoomed. Out from the blue sky – a lone Hun plane, like a hawk after its prey, and we were the victims. He missed us, but did not miss the poor old transport lines.

SKETCH OF A GERMAN PLANE ~ BY J.M. FRANCE. 1915.

THE MULES GO UP

BOMBED FROM THE AIR

Sketches by Jim Mautsaid

OUR FIRST EXPERIENCE OF AN ARIEL "STRAFE"

Out of the blue skies he swooped.

We were quartered in a little village.

Down like a flash..... dropped several bombs..... then zoomed away.

Our medical officer put several mules out of misery.

We view the ruins of our transport lines.

Like a speck in the sky, he disappears.

ONE OF OUR ANTI-AIR GUNS ON MOTOR TRACTOR IN ACTION – 1915.

Crash! Flash! Dust, smoke, and a blinding flame. Several bombs he let go, on his wild swoop over us. We shivered, the old billets shook, and he was gone! Our first aerial strafe was over. Bang! Bang! Bang! The anti-aircraft guns send scores of shells after him but, like a little speck in the sky, that black evil crossed machine sails away, home.

UP GO OUR MULES
Not a man hurt, but several mules were blown to bits and our medical officer put three or four more 'to rest'.

WINTER GARB. WARM – – – BUT A HIDING PLACE FOR 'CHATS'

Here's a YCV lad all dressed up.

GOOD – AND – BAD
Let me say right now they were warm, those goatskin jackets, but in a very short time became the home of our old enemy 'the chats' (a slang word for bugs, fleas, etc.) and nothing on earth would kill them. You could almost see that old skin coat moving about if you threw it down. After some weeks they became a hindrance and it was a bother to keep packing them for the transport wagons. The good points against the bad ones: this piece of kit was a washout and, truth to tell, we had no regrets when our old 'chatty' coats were withdrawn.

SLOGGING ALONG

JUST THE POOR B***** INFANTRY!

We slogged and then slogged again. Here today, gone tomorrow. Hamlets, villages, little towns all passed in film of vision. Some stand out; others tax the memory to remember. We must have covered thousands of miles on foot during our sojourn in France and Belgium. Bus travel, or rail travel, was unknown practically. I spent a stretch of ten months or so at one time and never once did my feet rest in a wagon or lorry. Yes! We could march some in those days.

Full fighting kit, that seemed to be constantly being added to, was always carried. How we carried it all often baffles me now. We marched in the snow, in the rain, and in the hottest days of summer, and at night too! The memory of some of those hikes still lingers. Did we, or were we used as a kind of bluff? A daylight trip from B------ to G----- ; a few hours' rest; then back on our tracks, or almost so. Did the enemy spies then report great movement of troops towards G-----? This was a suspicion of mine, or was it just to keep us 'fighting fit?' Sufferings were many. Sore and blistered feet, shoulders that were red and often chaffed, sickness and headache, not to mention utter weariness, but somehow we kept on our feet and just kept 'slogging along'.

How you felt after 30 kilometers slogging.

THE ROOKIES

THE ROOKIES.

FROM HOME
Straight in from base they came, a draft for the YCVs. In all my life I never heard such tales of all the horrors of war as these poor lads had to listen to. I felt sorry for some of the youngsters as their eyes bulged out in awe and bewilderment when listening to the deeds of daring; the rats grew as big as dogs, the shells fell like hailstones, stomachs were empty for weeks, and the Germans were over there (a shake of the thumb towards the firing line) in millions. In fact, it was impossible to live according to the 'tail swingers' (how they came through to tell the tale beats me) and, taking pity, I butted in with the remark 'Cut it out, it's not so bad my lads, so cheer up – you'll be all right'. Poor boys. Their turn came soon enough to face the music, and share our hardships, in this war business.

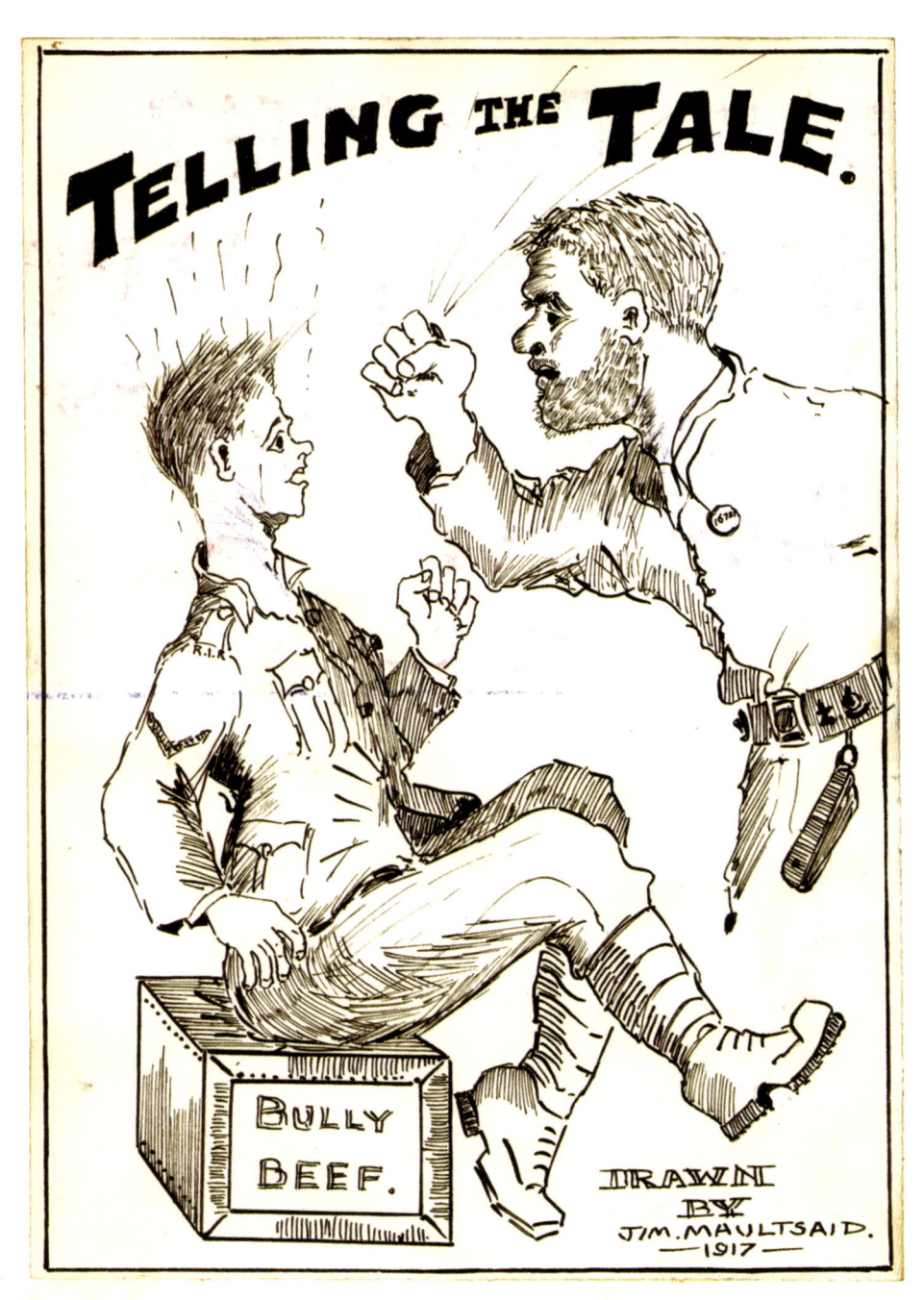

RATS THE SIZE OF—

GERMANS IN—

THE FAMOUS 29TH DIVISION

THE FAMOUS 29TH DIVISION.

SENT TO US FOR INSTRUCTION.

SUN HELMETS WERE OUT OF PLACE IN FRANCE.

J.M. 1916.

They came from Gallipoli and had made a great name out there but it was not the Turks that faced them now: it was Jerry.

Attached to the 36th Division for instruction, somehow they inferred to us that this was unnecessary and we let them 'go ahead'. Some of them actually got out into no man's land to collect nose caps and various souvenirs. We warned them to be careful, but mind your own business was written all over their faces in reply, so again we stood back and waited – waited to see Jerry teach them a lesson, and, by all the stars above, he sure did. Read the story later: 'Hell on Earth'.

Sketches ~ from ~ Real Life

Read about The Famous 29th Division.

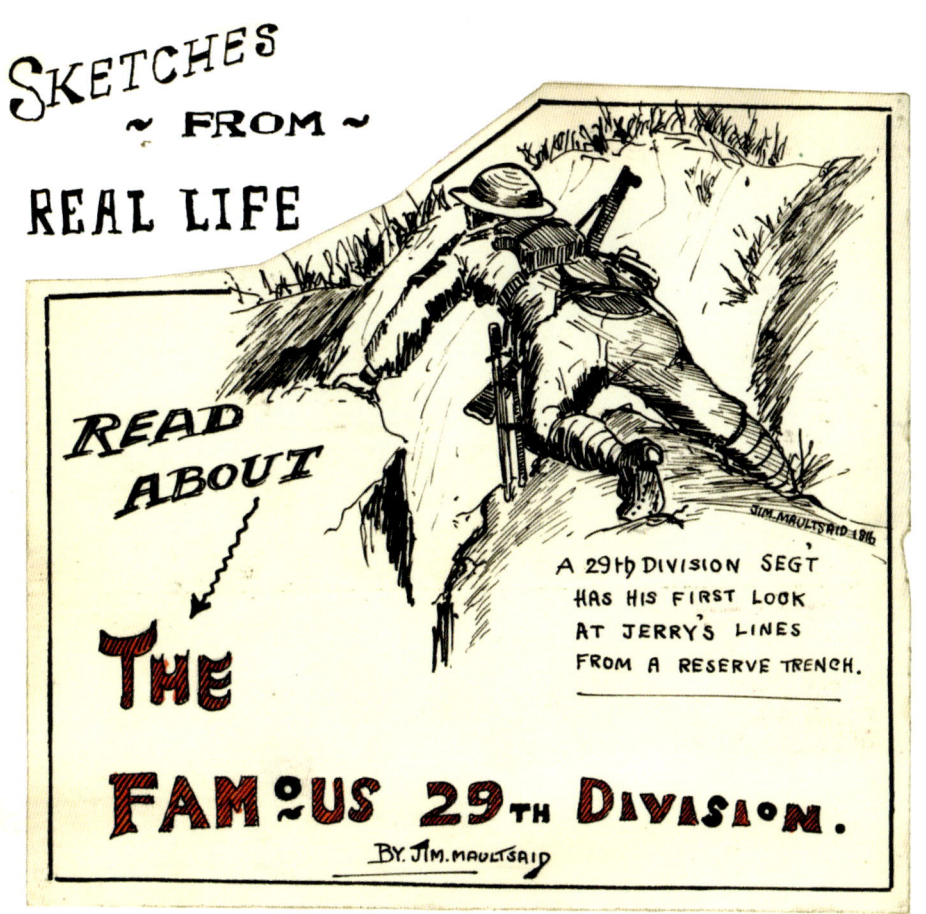

By Jim Maultsaid

A 29th Division Sergt has his first look at Jerry's lines from a reserve trench.

From Gallipoli.

The Warning!

We warned them it was not the Turks they were facing now. And —— "to cut out the souvenir stuff."

Jim Maultsaid — 1916 —

WE RAID THE MILL.
IT SAT IN THE SWAMP.
WE VIEWED IT FROM ALL ANGLES.
SEGT MAJOR DUQUEST AND I OFTEN HAD A DOZEN ROUNDS AT "THE MILL" – SIGHTS AT 1,000 YARDS.
PLANS WERE DISCUSSED.
SEGT MAJOR LOWERY. M.C LED THE RAIDING PARTY.
IN GOES THE BOMBS
DRAWN BY JIM MACLISAID. 1916.

WE RAID THE MILL

IN THE SWAMP
It sat out in the swamp and did not belong to us – or the enemy either: a bone of contention! We shelled it, we shot at it, and we suspected Jerry of taking possession at night-time to harry us with machine-gun fire. A raiding party was formed, led by Company Sergeant Major Lowry MC, plans laid and details worked out. I did not take part, much to my regret – it was not a D Company affair. To get at the old mill was a feat in itself as it was surrounded by swamp and very little dry land was visible.

ANXIOUS MOMENTS
'The' night arrives. Dark as pitch: off go the boys, bombs, revolvers etc. all complete. We wait in our trenches close by for the battle to start. Hours seem like years when to our ears came the sounds of bombs exploding; shots split the stillness of the night, then – stillness. Had we got in? Did we find any Jerries? Did any of our lads go under? Anxious eyes strained through the black night, awaiting the return, and praying that all were safe. Here they come! Ah! Hell, he was not there – not a dam German about the place. We had missed his visiting night!

HERE'S TO THE OLD COOKER CART

AN ARMY MARCHES ON ITS STOMACH
SO A FAMOUS GENERAL SAID
He was right! What we would have done without our old black box on wheels I don't know, and the cookhouse boys never let us down. Hail, rain, or snow, they never failed to send the hungry troops a dish of some kind. Soup may have been like tea, or tea tasted like soup, but it was warm, something to be thankful for. Difficulties were many that faced the staff of cookhouse lads. Sometimes food was short; it had to be divided evenly between four companies; perhaps the ration lorries were blown to pieces on the way up, or the potatoes lost, the bags of loaves dropped in the mud, or maybe water was scarce, and tea due in an hour or so! See them all black, all sweating, as they toiled amongst the pots, the dixies – and the steam – to get the grub ready for the boys in the line. See them below, resting from their labour to face our photographer, an off-duty moment.

WHAT WOULD WE HAVE DONE WITHOUT?

COOKS IN ACTION

Right up to the reserve line these wagons came. An old tumbledown house was converted into a kitchen – the smoke issues from the bowels of the earth itself – the 'cooks' have gone into action. A hole in the roadside ditch, the black box is pushed in, and from here comes the 'staff of life'. Grub! Grub! Grub!

ON THE MARCH

On the march that old chimney sends out volumes of smoke and soot as the black figure stokes up the fire and the cook 'cooks' for the troops.

CLEANLINESS IS NEXT TO

The little river flowed through the swamp – swift moving it was – and came right through our lines from Jerry's land. Our front line is not more than six or seven hundred yards away, but we were desperate for a real wash; not a dip in a tub, but a real splash! Off go the togs, and in we pop.

My! It's fine to feel the fresh water all over our verminous bodies (sorry to say it, reader, but we boys were simply 'walking away' at this time) and the soothing effect was wonderful. It was worth any risk, this bathe. Bathing pants are unknown; we plunge in, in nature's suit, and swim around.

A big shell bursts some fifty yards away, another roars over and goes slap into the water to send up a fountain of black water and mud but we pay not the slightest heed; this wash is far too precious. A dip! All my kingdom for a dip! We risked our very lives for one.

BATHING UNDER FIRE

Bathing in the Ancre just behind the front line

Drawn by Jim Maultsaid ~ 1916 ~

FROM THE HOME FRONT

Nothing was more looked forward to by the boys than mail from home.

LIKE CHILDREN
First rush was for the post when we got clear from our dirty straps and equipment, after getting out of the line. How we longed to see a letter or two; or listen for your name, to grab your parcel; or nothing to grab and how that heart of yours sank, sank down to your very boots, and a great empty feeling took possession of you! It was one of our great pleasures, looking forward like children for the post corporal; he was one of the most important men in the whole battalion.

IRELAND'S SATURDAY NIGHT
Did the Blues win? What about the wee Glens? Aye! And how did the Stripes [possibly a reference to Glentoran's strip] fare? Some of the lads have got a 'pink' [*Ireland's Saturday Night*, a now defunct sports paper, published in Belfast] and answer these eager questions as fast as a Lewis gun in action. Every scrap of the sports paper is read, then passed on to a chum. War! Trenches! Rats! Bugs! All forgotten. God bless the 'pink'.

LISBURN, PORTADOWN AND DONAGHADEE
Newspapers from Lisburn, Portadown, Lurgan and even Donaghadee sent a few of the boys back to their own home town, for an hour or so. It was wonderful how quiet the old billet became. Candles fluttered, spluttered figures crouched down in the straw. Eyes strained to read – read of home and loved ones – then out came writing pads and pencils to see a busy hour or so replying to these letters. Oh! How the 14th men wrote! Thousands of letters must have been penned weekly. It must have been a terrific strain on our poor platoon officers wading through all the 'stuff' turned out by the YCVs. Dear Minnie! Dear Mary! Dear Mother! Dear Dad! Oh! How weary they must have been.

ANY CAKE SERGEANT?
'Did she forget you this week Harry? I bet she has got a new boy and has forgotten you.' 'No cake this time, Sergeant? What's wrong?' Fun was poked, parcels shared out and then a rough voice said 'lights out'.

WE TAKE A CLOSE UP OF OUR GUNNERS

Strange as it may seem, we infantrymen got very few opportunities to see our own gunners in action.

ONE SUNNY DAY
Resting in Martinsart behind the Beaumont Hamel–Thiepval front one sunny day the sound of light field guns came to our ears, and no mistake they were fairly humming. The noise whipped the air as these quick-firing spitfires went crack! crack! crack!, hurling shells at some point in the enemy lines.

Up to this time my only view of our gunners actually firing had been shadowy ones at night-time as the flashes lit up the sky and half-naked figures jumped back into the gunpits to re-load and slam another shell into the night air. This was usually on the roadside, or from the edge of some little clump of trees, or again from amongst the ruins of some farmhouse buildings, but here at last was a chance to view the real thing – in broad daylight.

THE TREES SHOOK
Would the artillery officer object? Several of us slipped down the orchard, tree to tree and, locating the battery from the flashes and smoke rising on the still air, were soon within thirty yards or so of these little field guns.

My word, we enjoyed this novelty all unseen! Right before our eyes stood all four guns. Turn about they crashed out – and all the lot at once. Orders came thick and fast from the officer in command. The gunners, stripped to the waist, were sweating, the old orchard trees shook from concussion, and we forgot everything as we watched.

WE KNEW WELL
Fifteen or twenty minutes of this rapid fire, then, to our trained ears, came a sound well known to us. Screech – a rippling hiss and one of Jerry's shells fell in the trees some fifty yards away behind, to burst and send up a shower of clay and tree branches. Whizz! Whirr! Bang! Bang! Now we were in the very thick of an artillery duel.

The enemy guns had located our lot and it was a case of who 'went up' first. We flung ourselves down behind the trees for cover, but, fascinated, still kept our place and paid silent tribute to our friends the gunners.

FOUR GUNS THEN THREE
Hotter and hotter the battle grew, until the very earth was shaking and we could not tell the difference in our or the German explosions.

Would any of our guns catch a shell? Jerry was close now. Oh! My G**, he has got us! Right into the midst of one of our guns fell a shell – and, as the smoke cleared, figures covered with blood crawled out. Any killed? 'Come on Sergeant,' whispered a chum, 'let's go down and help.' 'No! No!' I replied, 'we have no earthly right here and will get court martialled if we interfere.'

THE GUNNERS.

A DUEL TO THE DEATH!
OUR FIELD GUNS IN ACTION AT MARIINSART!

At the bottom of an orchard we found the battery.

THIS or THIS

Dark figures by the roadside was our previous best.

NOW before our eyes in broad daylight was a light field battery of ours in action.

A sound we knew so well split the sky — and burst in the orchard — behind us.

THEN

Jerry now had the range — and plastered the orchard.

One gun out of action. We could hear the groans of the wounded gunners.

As I lay and watched I marvelled.

Drawn by Jim Maultsaid 1917

Three guns now could only reply. One was out of action. The sound of moans reached our ears as the poor wounded men lay in agony. So far as we could see, none were killed, but the whole gun crew was knocked out. The German fire slackened, fell away; so did ours, then both sides ceased, and we crawled away marvelling at the pluck of our boys 'the gunners'.

GUARDING THE SWAMP WASTES

This was the most unique term of trench duty that D Company had as yet encountered.

THE LITTLE RIVER ANCRE

As the good weather had more or less now set in, the swamp was gradually drying up. This would leave a big gap in our lines and I suppose the idea was to leave nothing to chance. I have already explained that the little river Ancre flowed through this waste marsh ground, and now our job was to take up position along the left bank of the river. At our rear ran the railway line; it also went through no man's land and was in working order on the German side behind Thiepval at or about Grandcourt. We often lay and listened to the engines as they puffed up and down with the rations, troops or supplies of war material during the night hours.

LITTLE PITS – OR SAPHEAD

The trench system was nothing like what we had been used to. Little pits were dug in the side of the bank, then narrow trenches ran out to end up in a little listening post that commanded a field of fire turning half left to face the front and across the swamp. But no enemy trenches were visible. Funny! What? Waiting and watching to avoid being taken by surprise.

Our only communication trench was the railway line; you just had to walk up the sleepers, then slip into the little trench and, lo!, you were on duty. It certainly was novel to us; we were so accustomed to the usual 'dug-in' feeling.

A DUD – FROM THE USA

A startled night bird flaps overhead. The little waves tumble over each other as they rush to join the river Somme down at Albert. A big water rat splashes in, and we half start up in surprise as the noise seems uncanny in this quiet night, and our eyes peer out to try and pierce the darkness. We curse a working party that noisily clatters along the narrow gauge railway running on the other side of the swamp. A big shell whines over to land splash in some soft spot and does not explode. One wag remarks, 'that one was made in the USA, I'm afraid' – a dud.

"Where we Lived" "Fought" and "Died".

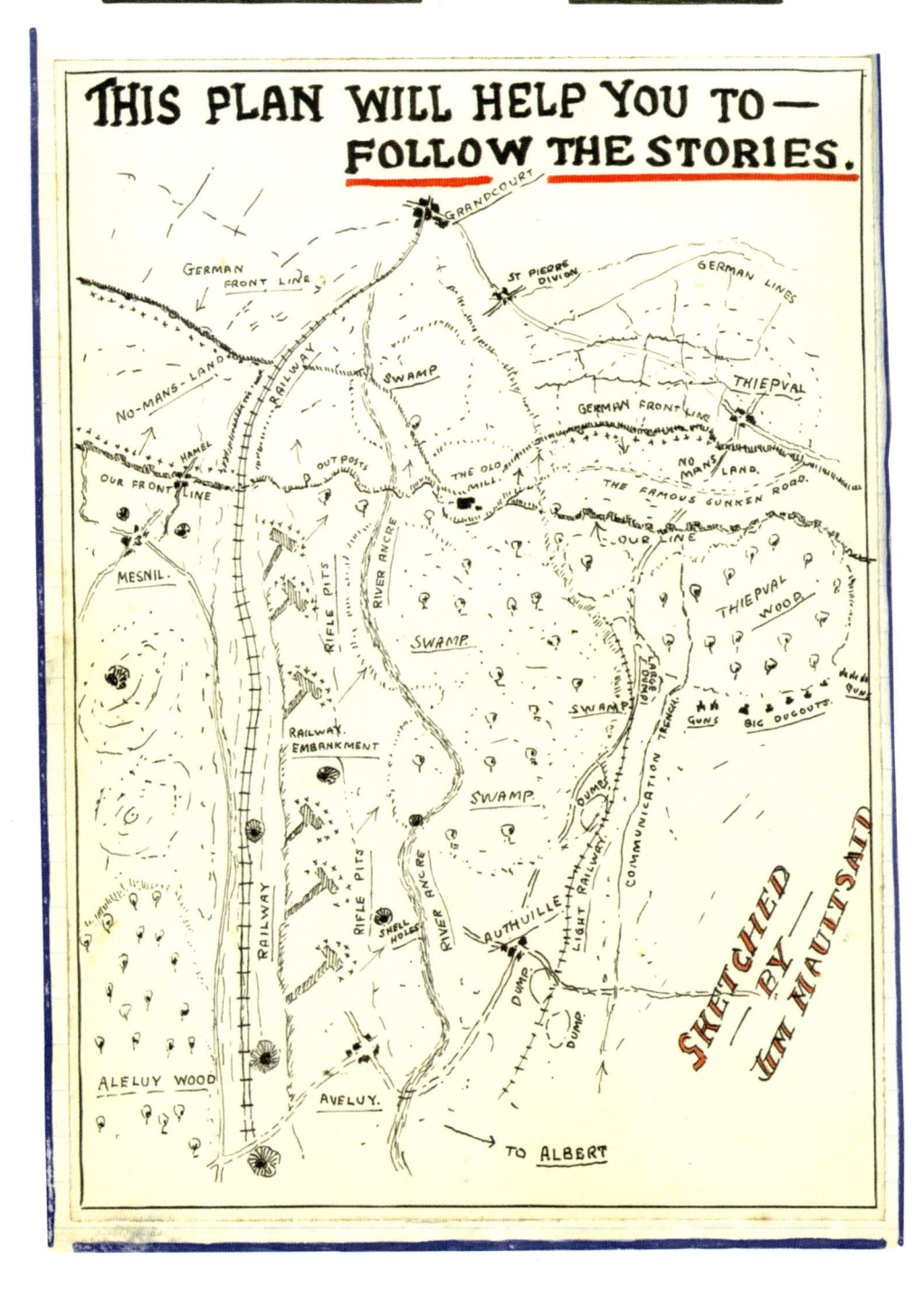

This plan will help you to — follow the stories.

Sketched by Jim Maultsaid

IN THE WOOD'S I SAT — AND SKETCHED!

TYPICAL GERMAN MACHINE GUNNER.

A FOREST HOME
IN AVELUY WOOD.

BUMBS

BULLY BEEF

BISCUIT STORE

BURIED TREASURE

FORGOTTEN?

STATLEY TREES

SAPLINGS

OLD FOREST KINGS.

AVELUY WOOD

BUILDING UP

ALL READY FOR THE LINE

A HEARTBREAK FOR FATIGUE SQUAD

UP THE LINE.

I DIG A GRAVE

I SLEEP SECURE.

A STORY IN PICTURES.

AVELUY WOOD

TO THE WOODS!
Yes! It was that right enough. The sky was our roof, and our home now was composed of big trees in full blossom. Stately trees! Little young saplings! Old and wizened giants of the forest, all side-by-side. I was in my element. I loved the forests, but this was no picnic; danger and death lurked overhead.

BURIED TREASURE
Working parties from dawn till dusk. Barbed wire, wooden stakes, tins of biscuits, bombs, shells, cartridges, bully beef, all the necessities for this terrible business of war was handled by us during our stretch of forest life, and that forest was honeycombed with bomb stores, food stores and all kinds of stores. I'll swear that I could go back yet and dig up stores that were never found – and still lie buried.

No single individual ever knew the full secrets of Aveluy Wood.

REVETMENTS
A task that loomed large during these days was making revetments, a trench support made from branches cut into lengths then knit together and bound with wire (see sketches). When completed these were stacked up and carted to the trenches by the troops during the night hours.

We became quite expert in making these supports, turning them out in fine style. It was a great change from ordinary fatigues, and was more or less enjoyed by the boys.

ZIP! ZIP! THROUGH THE TREES
After several nights in the wood we got a very unpleasant surprise. I woke up to hear the German machine-gun bullets slashing through the trees. It was a shock for us; we never dreamt we were under fire from rifle or machine-gun weapons. Sure enough, the bullets zipped – zipped – zipped; branches came tumbling down and we scrambled up to seek refuge behind big tree trunks – and spend the night crouching there trying to snatch a few hours' sleep. Jerry's gunners must have been resting all day as he was very active that night. We swore, we raved, we blasted him; but were glad to see the first rays of dawn creep through the treetops.

DIGGING A GRAVE
Having a brainwave, and fully determined to have some rest the next night, I set to after a mug of tea about 6.00pm and, much to the amazement of my chums, started to dig a grave for myself. Yes! A grave! 'What's the big idea, Sergeant? Getting ready for yourself?' Crude jokes were bandied about – at my expense; but wait, it was my turn to laugh.

As the grave was now some two feet deep I gathered leaves and bracken and covered the bottom as a covering and rest. It dawned on No 14 Platoon what the game was; then feverish activity to get a 'grave' dug for the night's rest.

DID IT WORK?

Did it work? You bet! It was fine beyond my dreams. Lying there in my 'clay box' I was safe and secure as Jerry raked the woods that night with his everlasting machine-gun fire.

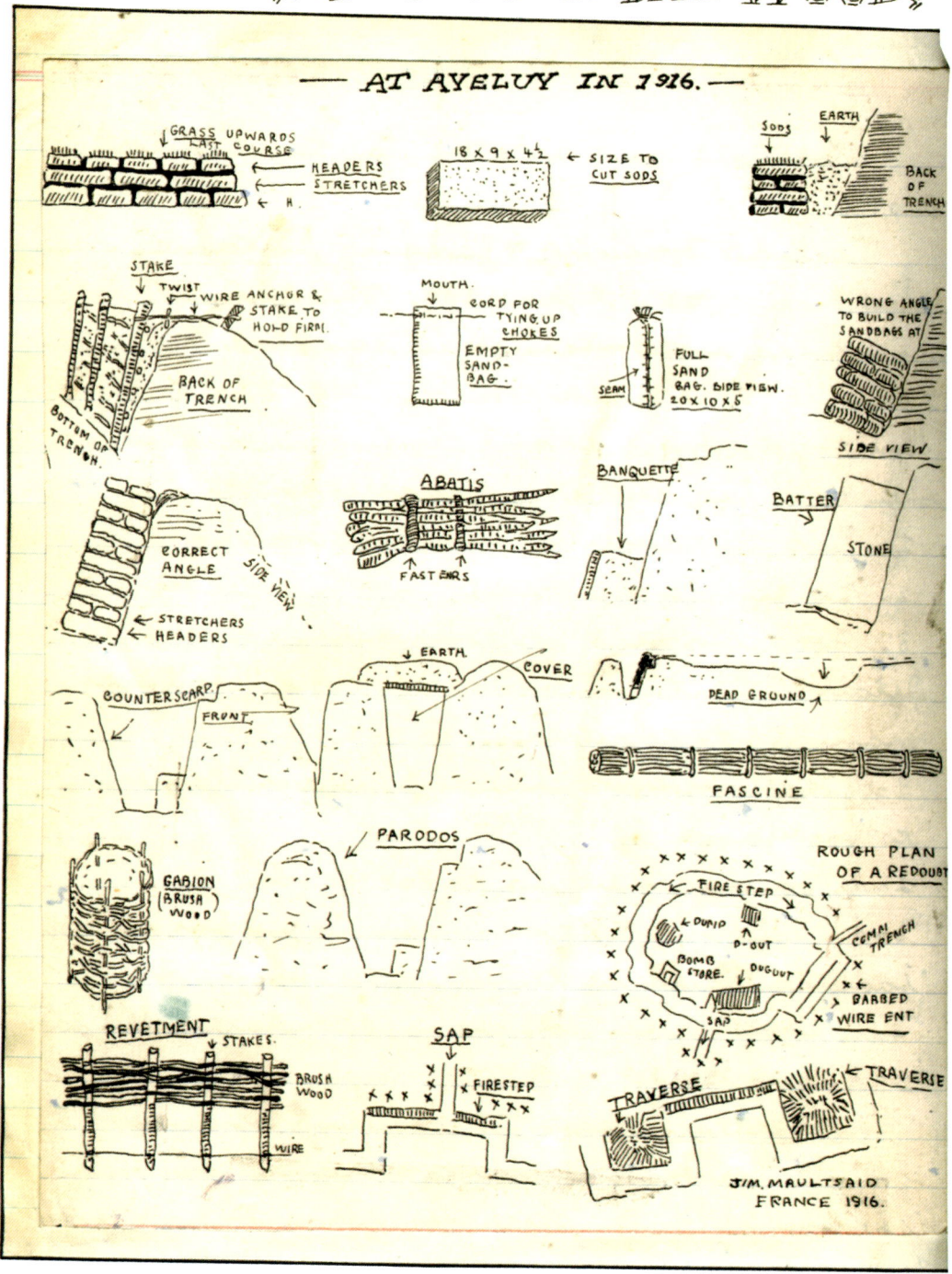

PRAISING THE LORD

THROUGH ALL OUR TROUBLES – WE DID NOT FORGET!
The Ulster Division boys were often kidded about carrying 'the little books of worship'. There was something in it too as practically every man had his 'book' in his pack, or pocket and every opportunity was taken to hold a service of some sort, no matter where we were. We had men in our lot of all creeds, and everyone had an avenue of the wildest description open to him to see that he did not forget to pay homage to God in his own way, and the men did not forget!

The YCVs had among their ranks men in hundreds that never forgot. At night, a little prayer! In the mornings, a few words. In the line, out from the line, at home, in fact all through the soldier's life these men gave praise! I can bring to mind a few of the boys that lived with God. Sergeant Kelly, John Towe, Joe Montgomery, Willie Reid and scores of others that I can say never took the Lord's name in vain; they lived a Christian life, ever looking upwards. Some of them have long since gone to that happy home they prepared themselves for and are now 'Safe in the Arms of Jesus'; no more worry, no more care! I hope to meet many, many of my wartime chums at that 'golden river' we often sang about – when 16,873 passes out, and Reveille sounds.

ONE IN A MILLION
I could not write this article and pass over a man in a million. He could come and cheer us in the front line, he cheered us in billets, he lived as we lived, sharing all our joys, our sorrows, just as much a soldier as us, yet one of God's own ministers: the Reverend Canon King, a Derryman [later Dean of Derry and Rector of Templemore], but one of us, he loved our Battalion, and we loved him. A man that was a real man; his good work will never be forgotten so long as a 14th Royal Irish Rifleman (YCV) lives. What more can I say?

YES! I HAVE DODGED (CHURCH PARADE)
Of course church parade in the army was a 'rite' and I don't mind confessing that I often missed a parade (on purpose) by volunteering for some fatigue or other. On the other hand, I often attended little meetings that had no official seal on them and felt all the better for it. Human nature to act like this, I suppose?

WE WERE NOT SAINTS
In times of distress I have cried to the good Lord for help and guidance for myself and my squad – and got an answer too – and by his grace was saved. At others, I have used his name in vain and been ashamed, but then soldiers were never saints; at least most of us were not. We were only human after all and the distress of a mighty war played many strange pranks on our general outlook on life. It left me a very broad vision.

16,873 ALMOST! WE HAD A SAYING

If your regimental number is on – it's for you!

It was not a healthy spot by any means. I should not have been so very inquisitive, but there you are; I just could not help looking through at the German line shining white in the sunlight. A great deal of sniping had been coming from 'across the way'. I was on the lookout for a sign of some kind, and the chance of a snap-shot at this 'pest', a pest that had already wounded several of our platoon.

CRACK! PLOP!

That bullet passed between a space of about six inches and smashed into a sandbag of hard chalk, not more than three inches from the side of my forehead. God! It was a narrow one. My hair stood on end as I jerked myself sideways and down! Too late, of course, if that bullet marked 16,873 had been true to its intended mark.

I had not got many seconds to study the lie of the land until I had been shot at, proof surely that Jerry had this part of our trenches well and truly 'taped'.

Revenge, and annoyance, flashed through my brain. Gathering several of the boys, I expounded a little plan. One of them placed an old biscuit tin on the top of his rifle, whilst three or four of us got to positions several yards away on each side of him, rifles at the ready and our eyes on the German front line, ready to spot 'the flash' from his rifle if he fell for our 'bait'.

BISCUIT TIN – AS 'BAIT'

Slowly up goes the biscuit tin! Crack! Crack! Two holes drilled through it – like a flash!

Did I see a red spurt of flame?

I'll swear I did – and my rifle spoke. Bang! Bang! Bang! Rapid fire! Our sharpshooters were now in action we pumped at least twenty rounds into that section of Jerry's line.

I could see the white chalk chips fly up around the parapet.

Moving further along our trench we all (about five of us now) took up new positions and crashed out a volley, up the spot we reckoned the trouble was coming from.

When no reply was received we gave up. One thing we showed our enemy and that was that we had no intention of sitting down to let him 'pot' us just when and how he liked. That was too much for Irish troops.

WELCOME IRISH RIFLES FROM JERRY

No wonder we made a new front on the Somme 'all alive'. One of the rifle battalions (the 10th) from Sandy Row and district had a notice stuck up in front of them once: 'WELCOME IRISH RIFLES'. Welcome! They shot it to pieces in reply!

SUMMER DAYS

WE REST TIRED BODIES – WE SEE NATURE AT ITS BEST
Withdrawn from the line for some ten days' rest, rest that was sadly needed to restore some life to tired bodies, wearied souls, never was a break so welcome. We had been in and around the battle front for months, never more than a few kilos from the everlasting shellfire that kept one awake o'nights, and had you on the stretch by day, ears on the alert listening for the wine of a big black 'coal box', or the rattle of a 'Jack Johnson', or, again, that never ending rat-tat-tat-tat-ping-zipp-zipp of the Hun sniper or machine gunner.

Now we were actually clear of it all and could breathe freely once more. Deep breathing, pure air, air that did not smell foul, and was free from that dankness and staleness that seemed to cling to us, even our clothes. It was the smell of death and desolation, it was putrid. Clear from it all for a little while. The Lord be praised.

SUNSHINE! LIFE!
Nature had been working, as she does in her quiet way, these few months past; gone were the drab winter days, the trees had new green and brown branches, the very earth itself seemed to smell sweet. Sunshine by day; life-giving sunrise, then sweet cool evenings.

Better to us than all the medicine in the world. We revived in spirit, we gathered new strength. It was good to be alive! Most of the usual routine stuff was gone through: smartness, general learning of the troops, route marches etc., etc.; but our officer commanding was a wise man and did not overdo it. It was a combination of work and play, then rest. We had time to go out on our own from the little villages for walks, or to explore the countryside – in fact 'fancy free'.

WHAT IS TO BE MY FATE?

I REST BY THE WAYSIDE

I loved to go out on my own to find a little forest, sit down, stretch my legs and think about the old homeland and the ones I loved. I watched the swallows, and wished I could fly away home, just for an hour or two. What thoughts! Would I live through this war? Would I lose an arm, or a leg, or both? I feared blindness and would rather die. Would I be killed? Would I, oh would I, ever get a loving thought sometimes from my friends of old?

Do you remember Jim Maultsaid? Ah! Poor old Jim!!! Yes! I would leave it all in God's hands. If he wanted me, well, I had to go, or perhaps my fate would be to still struggle on? I lay and thought all these things and then, to change my 'mind's wanderings', I would do a little sketch on the back of an old envelope; it was a wonderful tonic to me. I often wondered why I was not arrested as a spy, but of course this would have been ridiculous. Still they were suspicious in those days, and I might have landed myself in a bunch of trouble, but it never dawned on me like that, at the time.

ALL FORGOTTEN – IN FOOTBALL

Back in the billets, the boys have challenged No. 13 Platoon to a match. 'Will you play, Sergeant?' Would I play? Sure! Away we go, and forget all the worries of life and death in a full-blooded 'cup tie' football scrimmage.

FIGHTING FIT

KEEP MILLING JIM

News drifted through that there was to be a brigade sportsday held in the near future and boxing championships would figure on the programme as well as the usual track events. Now I had my eye on the nine-stone championship belt of 109 Brigade. Here was my chance. My old friends Jim McGee (heavyweight) Tommy Rosbotham (lightweight) and M. McMurray (middleweight) had their minds set to assist me in my ambition, so we set about the training business. The gloves soon made their appearance (far too big for me) and down to 'hard tack' got we, us and co.

The day's toil over, a little rest, then stripped for the fray and three rounds each with my partners – getting my fighting eye in; no slapping with open gloves here, it was 'all-out'. Big Jimmy Magee made me punch him just as hard as I could and he did not strike back, just dodged around. Now Jim, Tommy and you have a go.

Chums as we were meant nothing. We simply slashed into each other. It was fierce going. Jim shot a stream of advice at me as I made a miss, or said 'good' if I cut Tommy a smart one.

Shadow boxing was my own idea (you fought your own shadow); very little physical jerks required and I was as fit as a man could be. About a week or so of this and, oh my, I was in great form. The bouts were to be four-round affairs of two minutes each; we worked on this. I got a nice black eye from McMurray, but this did not worry me much. I was ready to box for the honour of the YCVs. Lots of the boys took a great interest in our training and tendered advice good and bad.

OUT FOR HONOURS

The hundred yards, the two hundred and twenty yards, and the relay race made a great appeal to me also and I trained for these events too. How did I do it all? Looking back, it baffles me now to know where I got the staying power to attempt all this? Of course I had been an athlete all my life, did not drink or smoke, was always in 'fighting fit form', then the hard life; this is the answer, I suppose.

FIGHTING FIT.

BIG JIM MAGEE ACTS AS A PUNCH BAG.

SHADOW BOXING IN THE SUN.

JIM.MAULTSAID

THE TROOPS ENJOYED "THE MILLING"

A ROUGH RING ERECTED READY FOR ROUND ONE

← NOTE STARS & STRIPES ON BELT

READY TO BOX
FOR THE HONOUR of the Y.C.V's.

CHANGE HERE!

NO STATIONS, BUT WE HAD OUR LITTLE JOKE
Alongside the swamp a little light railway swept right up to the front line almost under the covering of trees and wildlife that abounded on this part of the Somme front. It was used by us to carry all kinds of war supplies to Thiepval wood and it was usually operated during the night hours by the troops – no engine, just good old manpower.

NEILL'S HILL, SAINTFIELD
Stand clear there and let the Bangor Express have a through run! Some wag had taken the time and pains to paint several signboards with the names of famous stations on the BCDR [Belfast and County Down Railway] route: NEILL'S HILL, BALLYMACARRET HALT, SAINTFIELD etc. These were stuck up at about two hundred yards distance apart. Made in fun, [they] somehow gave me a 'homely feeling'. It was a touch of 'home' out here, and enjoyed by the troops.

BACK TO MY OLD TRADE
Fourteen Platoon were now operating this front-line railway. Being a railwayman since boyhood, I had now got a job at my own trade. What?

LET'S GET TO H*** OUT OF THIS
Little trucks were loaded up by us at the dump, then 'all clear sounded' and away we went, but it was three men to each bogie *pushing* the goods wagons. Our cargo was a pit prop for dugouts, wire for the stakes in no man's land, boxes of ammunition for the troops, but no rum jars or passengers. Running into Neill's Hill, a bogie jumps the track, the next one bashes into the operations in front up in a heap – and over goes the whole outfit.

The noise and the cursing is not fit for a respectable railway station, and the clatter made I'm sure is heard by the Germans. 'Shut up! You d*** fools,' I whisper. 'Dry up Bowden! Give a hand here Rooney and Black! Blast your legs! Let's get to h*** out of this, or we'll be here all night.'

SWISH! CRASH!
Swish-swish-crash! Crash!

TAKE YOUR FEET OFF MY FACE!
Like a flash we throw ourselves right into the communication trench that fortunately runs beside us as two big shells come smashing down on us. Showers of rubbish bounce off our steel hats. We gasp for breath and wait. Black smoke floats down to us, thick choking stuff; we still hug the earth. 'Anyone hurt?' 'Are you there Jackson?' 'Take your big feet off my face Kelly!' 'Who owns this arm?' All mixed up, tied in knots, at last we scramble back to find a bogie gone – gone up in smoke! And about six yards of line missing. What a nice big deep shell hole right in the middle of our little railway.

Here's a mess now! Come on, unload the trucks, dump the stuff out and carry the bogie wheels and all around the big hole, load up and push along.

CHANGE HERE!

NEILL'S HILL

SOME WAG HAD PUT UP A SIGN-BOARD LABELLED NEILL'S HILL

RUNNING INTO NEILLS HILL A BOGIE JUMPS THE TRACK — THE NEXT ONE BASHES INTO IT. WHAT A DIN!

THE ULSTER DIVISION BOYS SHOULD REMEMBER THIS FAMOUS SPOT?

HERE'S THE LITTLE RAILWAY AT BACK OF THIEPVAL WOOD. THE ULSTER DIVISION BOYS WILL ALL KNOW THIS FAMOUS SPOT?

FRONT LINE
FOREST
SENTRY
DUGOUTS
ENTRANCE TO ELGIN AVENUE
SHELL HOLE
PUMP
SWAMP
LIGHT RAILWAY
COMMUNICATION TRENCH
BOGIE

JIM. MAULTSAID. 1916.

WAITING ON THE W-H-I-N-E
This put the damper on us and no error. Quietly now we trundled on, holding our breath, ears as sharp as sharp can be – to catch the whine of an 'aerial express', but none came.

WE SLIDE BACK TO BELFAST
Our stock delivered at the 'railhead', the return journey completed, I sigh a deep one of relief as we slide into BELFAST.

STORM TROOPS FIERCE TRAINING

FOR 'THE DAY'
Withdrawn from the immediate battle zone, it was 'training intense'. From whispered words, it was now openly discussed: the *big push* that we, the British armies, were to make against the German lines sometime early this summer. This news was more or less welcome as we were fed up with the trench business of always standing and just taking all that came to us. Glory be! We were to get a real crack at 'Jerry' – and by heavens we would show him a thing or two. As man to man we had no fear of his best troops. All we wanted was the chance. Now it was in the air: that the 36th Division were to get it.

PLANS STUDIED
Plans of our sector (that we were to attack) were in the hands of our headquarters, each Battalion had its own objective laid down and we actually dug skeleton trenches and marked out the various enemy strongpoints by white tape markings stuck up on sticks.

ALL FOR THE 'DAY'
These points were attacked by us, again and again. We studied, we fought our battle against the dummy lines, we charged, we shot, we killed hundreds of the enemy – all in imagination. It was work, hard work too from morning till night. No doubt about it; we were to be 'storm troops' to shock the Huns, and never was there a fitter Battalion than the 14th Royal Irish Rifles for this piece of work. Like greyhounds, trained to the minute, all ready for the 'off', could 'Jerry' stop us? I felt sure he could not, provided we got at him, in his lair. We depended on our guns clearing a path for us; we would do the rest.

OUR JOB WAS
As a bomber my job was to clear out the dugouts and attack the strongpoints with my squad.

It was reckoned to give us a great deal of trouble. This bit of the line was carefully dug in full detail by us: wire defences put up, then we bombed from all positions; real bombs were used. Dummy figures even were placed in the trenches (bags of grass etc.) to represent the Germans. We slung all kinds of hand grenades at these, then noted the effect of our fire.

Practice in the art of getting up supplies of bombs, the bringing forward of reserves to fill the gap, the length of our throwing, the accuracy, was all studied; and we improved wonderfully in all these departments. But how we put our heart and soul into the business.

A FEW PAGES OVER - YOU CAN

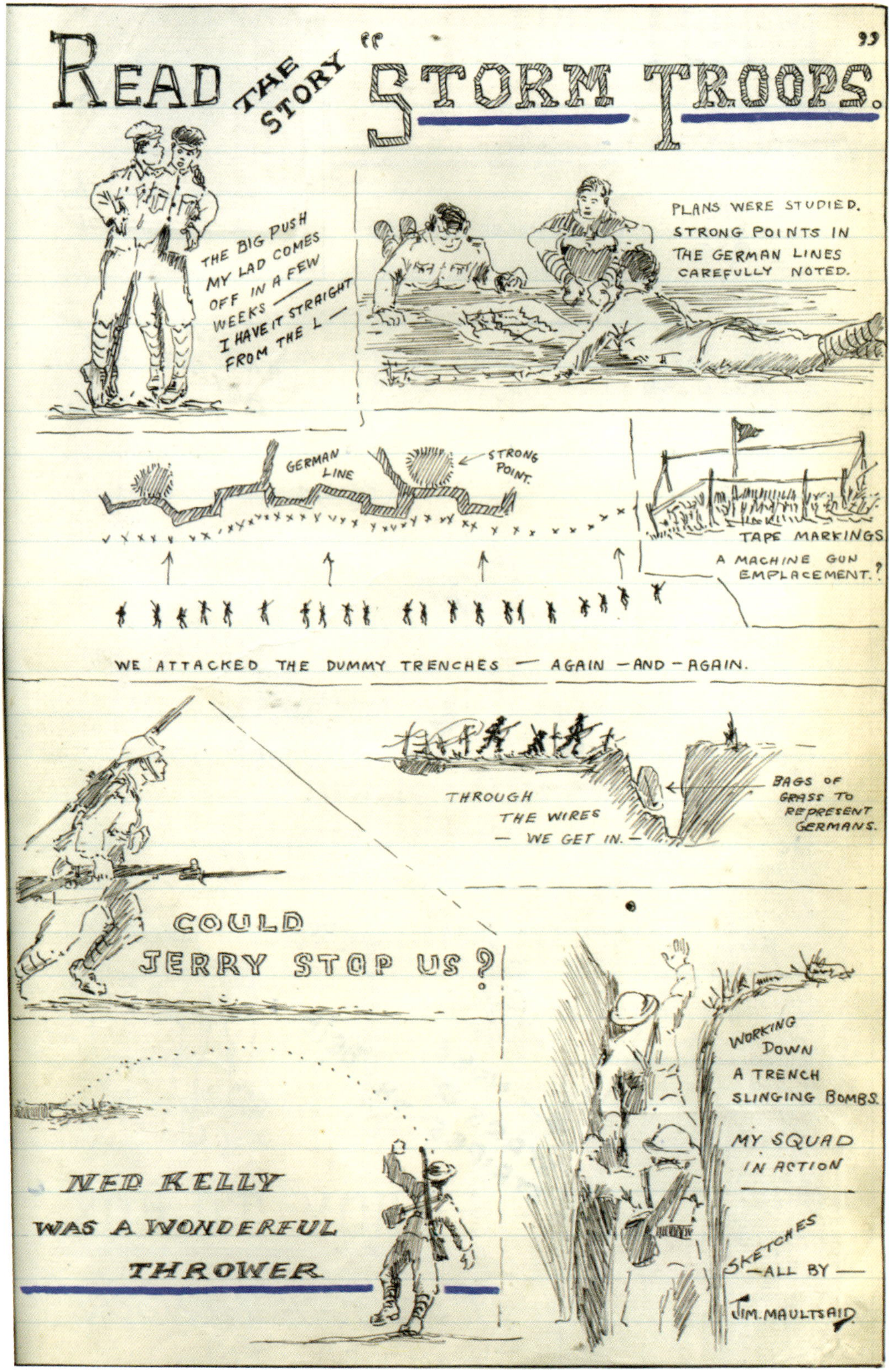

Mind you, we had no delusions. It was going to be a tough job, as it was said that this part of the German line was 'untakeable' and the strongest section on the Western Front. Could we wrest it from him?

Well! We would make a d*** good try anyhow!

YES! WE COULD THROW

I had some wonderful bomb throwers in my section. One in particular, his name was Ned Kelly (not in any way related to the famous bushranger), could throw a Mills bomb a good fifty yards and more – and hit the circle! Yes, he could sling those bombs.

THE BIG CHIEF

WHERE GOOD BOMBERS CAME FROM

Well away from the battalion headquarters, my squad and I were out on a bombing practice; they did not like us knocking around when we were 'taking the pins' away and letting the deadly little Mills bombs fly. We were nicknamed the 'suicide club', 'sure death' squad, etc., etc.

RISKING OUR LIVES

Bang! Bang! Fresh as paint, we were in great form. Right into the pit at every turn almost, we were dropping our deadly missiles. Every man was a crack thrower. Months of weary practice had brought perfection. Our latest stunt was letting the pin out, counting 'one, two', then throwing the bomb. It took about five seconds roughly to explode the bomb, so we were now knocking two seconds off, taking our lives in our hands. A slip, and up all of our little lot would have gone! Not careless, but a little reckless.

Over the rising ground they came. A body of horsemen.

Dashing right up behind us these strangers drew rein, and I looked at their badges Inniskilling Dragoons. Irishmen! Yes! Lances and all in complete array, and the red caps! Rank was here!

'Are you in charge, Sergeant?'

'Yes, Sir!'

'What is your regiment?'

'The Fourteenth Royal Irish Rifles, Sir!'

'A bombing squad?'

'Yes, Sir, out at practice.'

'Good! Let me see you throw a bomb yourself.'

'Keep back please, these are real-life bombs.'

A BULL'S EYE
I throw a beauty! Right into the pit some forty yards away. Nervous? Yes! I was, but full of confidence, and luck was on my side. 'Very good, Sergeant! Now let me see your men throw.' I picked my 'crack' throwers. Bang! Bang! Bang! All bull's-eyes. I was delighted. 'Splendid work, Sergeant!'

The speaker's face was somehow not unknown to me. Where did I see it before? My heavens! It's -------- himself. I almost collapse, but maintained an outward calm that I did not feel.

ALL IRISHMEN?
'Are your boys all Irishmen, Sergeant?'
'Yes Sir! All from Belfast.'

YES! YES!
'Yes! Yes! I see now why you're all such good bombers.'

I SEE THE REASON
'From Belfast – you should all be good at this game.'

FAREWELL
I smiled, saluted again and the *big chief* and his escort moved off at a sharp trot.

SIT DOWN MY LADS
'Sit down my lads, that's enough for today. Did you know that was the great Sir Douglas Haig, our Commander-in-Chief that has just passed by?' Gasps of astonishment from the troops. 'Lord, if I had known that,' says Rogers, 'I would have dropped "a pill" in sheer fright, and, and killed us all.'

I WAS SURPRISED
This was to be my one and only close-up of our leader during my army career. A fine inspiring figure of a man. Well groomed. Just like a figure out of a bandbox. But his face! I got a shock. To me it looked as if it was, or had been, powdered.

HELL ON EARTH

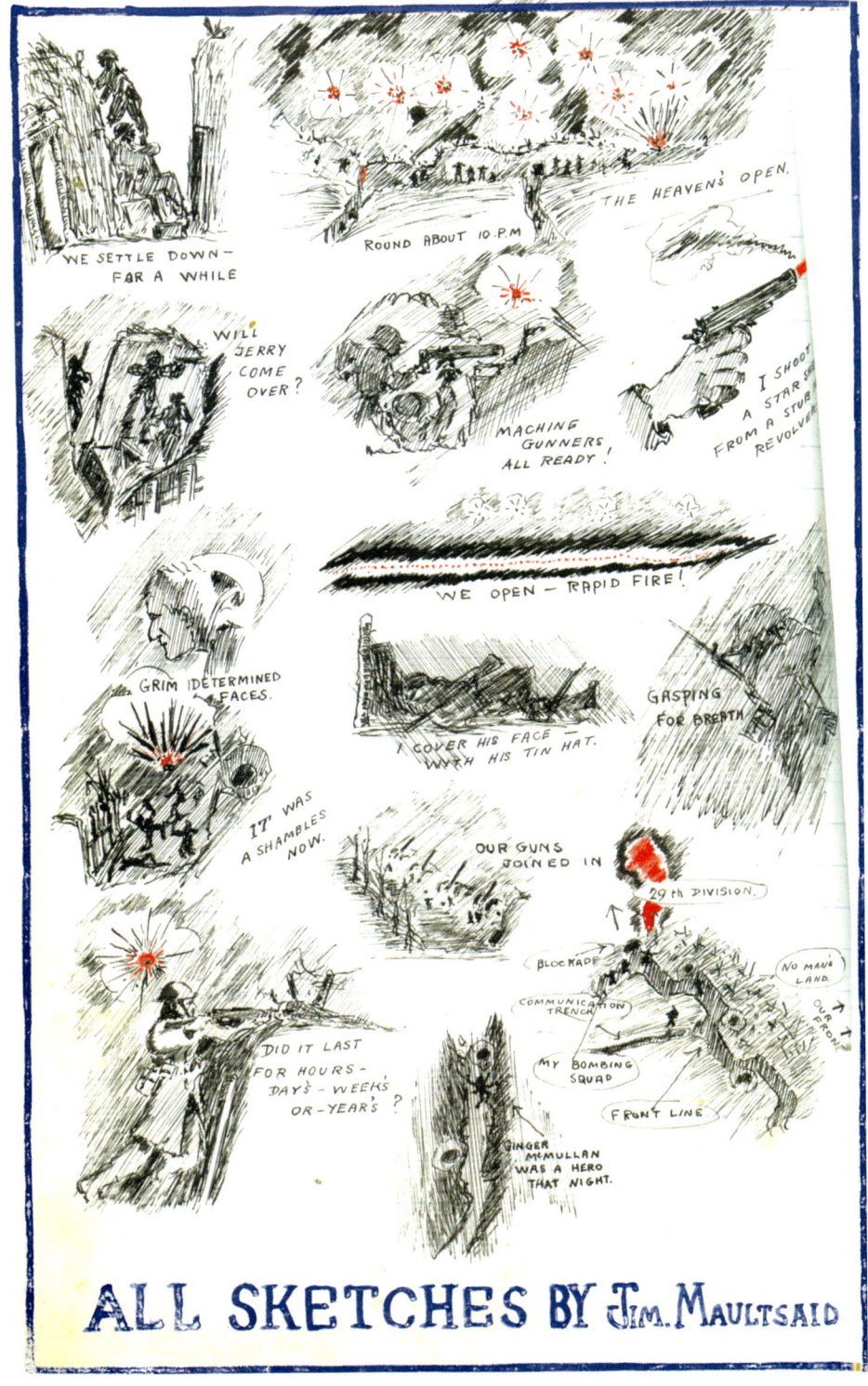

WE PASS THROUGH A TERRIBLE ORDEAL AND 'STAND FAST'.
MENTIONED IN DIVISIONAL ORDERS

One of the most awful nights our boys ever experienced up to this time (6 May 1916) left us all limp and nerve racked. It was simply a sight of 'hell' for several hours; and there is not a 14th man alive today that passed through this ordeal who cannot 'live' this night all over again.

SEE THE TORN PAGE

Read the page, torn from my little notebook, and you, no doubt, can read between the lines and sum up the agony we passed through.

WE SETTLE DOWN FOR A WHILE

'All quiet.' Yes! Too d*** quiet for my taste. We settle down on a real summer's night to our guarding of the front-line trenches opposite Beaumont Hamel. The 29th Division was on our left (you read about this lot earlier in the book); they were now holding a section of the line themselves.

THE HEAVENS OPEN!

Somewhere round about 10.00pm 'the heavens opened' a perfect hail of shells, all at once, into the 29th Division trenches. The very ground we stood on rocked and swayed. What a roar! What a sight! But not our turn yet. Stand to! Stand to! Man the trenches! Figures came tumbling out from little trenches. Belts were hurriedly adjusted – and the YCVs were all at their 'stations'.

IS JERRY COMING?

Half left we faced. An attack was feared, up go our coloured lights, fired from a short snub-nosed revolver, and they fell into no man's land, lighting up the scene in many colours. I load, and fire, my own 'star shell' gun several times.

WHERE WAS THE 29TH DIVISION?

We lose touch with the right of the 29th Division. Is Jerry raiding their trenches? Here's a mess! 'Sergeant Maultsaid,' Lieutenant Monard roars into my ear. 'Yes! Sir.' 'Get your bombing section and take up position on the left of our Battalion in case the enemy try to rush us.' 'Come on boys, follow me!' We dash to the left. I halt the boys and post them in favourable positions to stem the tide, if it comes our way. He won't take us on our flank without a fight. Not tonight anyhow!

RAPID FIRE! TO HELP OUR CHUMS

'Fire! Rapid fire!' comes the order, and the YCVs opened up. Like a thousand angry bees, our bullets swept the enemy trenches. Machine guns, Lewis guns and rifle fire crashed out, swelling to a din that made the head ache. We would do our best to save our chums from Gallipoli. Crash! Crash! Crash! Blinding smoke and fumes. He had switched his gunfire over to us. Now we were for it.

What a mighty load of metal is smashing down, red hot iron hissing through the air. My very breath leaves me for a few seconds as that awful tornado sweeps over us. Could human beings stand up to this – and live?

WE LIVE 'IN HELL'
Hotter and hotter it grew. Our trenches seem to be on fire. It was raining shells. Shells of all sizes, swishing past, bursting in front, bursting above us, and behind. The wire defences were going up, sandbags scattered, big gaping ugly holes that reeked poison – and flames! God! Above it was 'hell', if ever such a place was – or is! And at its worst!

I'M COVERED IN BLOOD
'Ah Jim! I'm done!' 'Hold up chum.' I step down – and the warm blood of a pal splashes all over me as I grasp him and bear his weight in my effort to lower him gently down. Poor boy; 6 May 1916 was his last day on this earth. I place his tin hat right over his face and jump back to my place on the fire-step. Captain Willis is by my side. 'Can we not go over, Captain, and get at those b★★★★★★★?' I cry out! My nose bleeds. I'm smothered in blood. 'Keep it up, boys,' I yell! 'Give them h★★★.'

It was a furnace now. A shambles! Battered traverses: rifles, picks, shovels, logs of wood, and the bodies of our chums all mixed up, in a welter of confusion.

GRIM DETERMINED FACES
Ammunition was running short. Boxes were dragged up from the reserve dump and we blazed away. The explosion of a huge shell sent several of us crashing back all in a heap. We gasp! We choke and splutter, and jump in again to our place in the line. Would the boys 'stand fast?'

Never did I see such grim determined faces! 'Wish to G★★ he would come over, Sergeant, and let us get a crack at him,' shout two or three of my platoon; and I wish to G★★ he had. It would only have been over our dead bodies he would have passed. We would have died fighting!

HOLDING ON – TO 'THE LINE'
Our guns joined in. We had long since sent back an SOS signal for their help. And we got it, such as it was – nothing compared to the Huns. They raked us, they battered us, and our trench system was in smithereens. But we 'held on'.

HOURS – DAYS – WEEKS – OR YEARS?
Hours of this. Or was it days, or weeks? I knew not, it seemed like years to me. Then the storm died down. Gradually died away, and all was quiet once more, east of Thiepval.

DOWN! DOWN! DOWN!
A night of nights. Long to be remembered. A disturber of sleep. One that gave you dreams, that startled you: to wake up and find yourself sweating, all of a wetness, and a mind that was still spinning round, or crashing down! Down! Down!

GINGER McMULLEN- A HERO

Ginger McMullen (the famous Ginger) played a part this night that he never got any official award, or mentioned for. He went away out, and up the trenches again and again looking for the right hand man of the 29th Division – and did not find him. He was all alone. In a world of his own amongst the bursting shells, at a time when human company was more precious than gold. Ginger was a hero that night – and a soldier!

THE END